Dharma in the Golden State

The Religious Contours of California
Window to the World's Religions

A nine-volume series co-edited by
Phillip E. Hammond and Ninian Smart
DEPARTMENT OF RELIGIOUS STUDIES
UNIVERSITY OF CALIFORNIA, SANTA BARBARA

Dharma in the Golden State

South Asian Religious Traditions in California

CYBELLE T. SHATTUCK

Volume IV of
The Religious Contours of California
Window to the World's Religions

A PROJECT OF
The Center for the Study of Religion
University of California, Santa Barbara

IN ASSOCIATION WITH
The California Historical Society

FITHIAN PRESS
SANTA BARBARA • 1996

Copyright ©1996 by the University of California Regents
All rights reserved
Printed in the United States of America

Design and typography by Jim Cook

Published by Fithian Press
A Division of Daniel & Daniel, Publishers, Inc.
Post Office Box 1525
Santa Barbara, California 93102

LIBRARY OF CONGRESS CATALOGING-IN-PUBLICATION DATA
Shattuck, Cybelle T.
    Dharma in the golden state: South Asian religious
traditions in California / Cybelle T. Shattuck.
        p.   cm. — (Religious contours of California; v. 4)
    Includes bibliographical references and index.
    ISBN 1-56474-175-3 (pbk.: alk. paper)
    1. South Asians—California—Religion.   2. California—
Religious life and customs.   3. Asia, South—Religion.
I. Title.   II. Series.
BL2527.C2S53   1996
294'.09794—dc20   96-5268
                                                            CIP

Contents

1 South Asian Dharma Comes to the Golden State

Dharma is the Indian word for religion. It also means duty, law, moral behavior, and virtuous living. Religion as *dharma* implies socio-ethical laws and obligations that are part of the South Asian cultural milieu. Thus, religion informs the approach to daily activities, social interactions, and the sense of how one is supposed to live on a day-to-day basis. Transferring the actions and ideals that make up a dharmic life to a new cultural setting is a challenge. The magnitude of that challenge was not immediately apparent to the first South Asian immigrants who arrived in the United States because they were focusing on survival and establishing economic security. As they began to start families, however, finding ways to practice *dharma* and to teach their traditional values to their children in a strange culture assumed new importance.

California is indeed the Golden State for the South Asian immigrants who have made the Pacific Coast their home. They have come here seeking economic opportunity from India, Pakistan, Sri Lanka, Tibet, and intermediary countries in the Caribbean and Africa. Some came alone with the intention of working for a few years to earn money and then returning to their families overseas. Others, who came in search of professional careers because they were well-educated but had few opportunities to use their knowledge and skills in South Asia, brought their families with them. Whether or not they intended to stay in the United States permanently, they have become one of the fastest growing immigrant populations in the nation. As this South Asian community grows, it is working to transfer the elements of cultural identity to its new setting. One of the most visible signs of this new presence is the growing number of temples, *gurdwara*s, mosques, and South Asian community centers across America. In these places of worship traditional celebrations strengthen the community and educate the next generation. And here, too, the dynamism of religion is evident in the adaptations these new Americans are making to preserve and pass on their *dharma* in modern American society.

History of South Asian Immigration to California

Although there were isolated cases of single immigrants from South Asia before the twentieth century, only in the last one hundred years has there been a real migration. There have been two waves of South Asian immigrants. The first lasted from the turn of the twentieth century to the mid-1920s, and the second, which began after 1965, is still under way. Many of the South Asians from the first migration returned to India to fight for independence, and others left periodically because the United States instituted anti-Asian policies on immigration and citizenship. The second wave of immigrants began after these laws were changed and constrictive immigration quotas removed.

During the first twenty years of this century, almost 7,000 Indians immigrated to the United States. Most of these were Sikhs from the Punjab. They obtained work as manual laborers, first in the lumber industry on the west coast, and then in agriculture. A few professionals and businessmen, mostly Hindu and Muslim, settled in San Francisco, Los Angeles, New York City, and in the Midwest. From 1908 to 1920 there was also an annual average of 125 Indians in the country on temporary visas, often as students.

In rural California, Sikhs took work as farm laborers in the Imperial, San Joaquin, and Sacramento valleys. Most of these workers were young men who had come to earn money to send home to their families in India. Some returned to India, but those who remained pooled their resources and became tenant farmers in the valleys of central California, where many of them were very successful. After 1906, Indians were barred from U.S. citizenship on the ground that they were not white, a decision which was confirmed by the Supreme Court in the Thind case of 1923. This made land ownership in California problematic, although most South Asians were able to circumvent the law by having other people's names put on their deeds.

Between 1920 and 1940, 4,500 Indians returned to India. Many had come only to make money and returned to India when their families no longer needed their absentee income. Others found life in an intolerant America too difficult. In the early 1940s there were only about 2,400 Indians in the United States, 1,400 of whom were in California. By 1946 the entire Indian population of the U.S. had decreased to fewer than 1,500 persons. These workers, scattered across the state in small groups and separated from their families, were slowly losing their cultural and religious traditions.

The year 1946, however, marked a major change in U.S. immigration policies. The government established an annual immigration quota of 100 persons for Indian immigration and made Indians eligible for naturalization. Although only 6,000 Indian immigrants were admitted in the next twenty years, these new migrants were very different from the single laborers coming over to work in the first decades of the century. For the first time, brides could be brought over from India, families could be reconstituted, and American land could be owned with a clear title.

It was India's imminent independence from British rule that was most directly responsible for this change in American government policy. The U.S. could hardly expect to establish diplomatic relations with a free India while excluding Indian citizens from American soil. Independence also changed the immigrant community in two ways. The new open policy caused rapid increase in the number of migrants and made it possible for whole families to relocate. But the partition of Pakistan from India that accompanied independence brought a less positive legacy. The small community of Indian immigrants in the United States during the first part of the century had not segregated themselves from each other on the basis of religious divisions except in worship. Muslims, Hindus, and Sikhs had generally viewed themselves as Indians, sharing a cultural-historical heritage that linked them together in a foreign (and often inhospitable) land. The partition of India divided South Asians according to religious tradition, making it less acceptable for members of different faiths to share cultural activities. As the number of immigrants grew, the immigrant population began to include not only women and children, for whom it was important to maintain traditions intact, but also people with bitter memories of the bloody strife that accompanied the partition. Thus the different Indian groups came to place more emphasis on their separate identities and less and less exhibited the unity that had characterized the first wave of Indian immigrants.

The number of migrants coming to America from South Asia jumped dramatically after the Hart-Cellar Act of 1965 abolished the national-origins quota system and ended the outright exclusion of people from the Asia-Pacific Triangle. The eastern hemisphere of the world was allowed 170,000 immigrants annually with a limit of 20,000 from each country. Preferential treatment was to be given to immediate family members and highly trained professionals such as engineers, physicians, scientists, professors, teachers, and business-men. The total annual quota has gone up since, and there have been numerous exceptions that have made it possible for people to be admitted even after the quotas were full (e.g. close family ties).

The new wave of immigrants is, therefore, quite different from the first group. These migrants are predominantly from urban areas and usually settle in urban areas in America. In 1980, U.S. census figures showed 387,223 Asian Indians in the United States, 60,000 of whom were in California, mostly residing in Los Angeles and San Francisco. By 1990, California was the home of 160,000 South Asians.

As the size of this South Asian community grows, the diverse religious traditions that these new Americans bring with them are beginning to become more visible. There is, for instance, a beautiful Hindu temple in Calabasas, several miles north of Los Angeles, built in the traditional architectural style of south India, and smaller tem-ples can now be found in a dozen California cities. There are Bud-dhist temples and Muslim mosques all across the state, some tradi-tional and others indistinguishable from the surrounding suburban buildings. Sikhs no longer need to travel to the original *gurdwara* (religious center) in Stockton (established in 1912) for festivals, because they now have local *gurdwara*s. Jains gather in their own centers and private homes. In addition, South Asian Muslims, Christians, Jews, and Zoroastrians have found welcome in the mosques, churches, synagogues, and centers of their international brethren. All these traditions have become an integral part of the religious landscape in California in the late twentieth century.

History of South Asian Religion

The South Asian religious traditions that we see among the people coming to the United States today are the result of nearly 5,000 years of growth, change, assimilation, and accretion of all the different ideas and practices that have been melded in the cultural basin of the Indian sub-continent. It is not possible to give more than a brief overview of this religious history here, but the following account will address the major developments.

There was an urbanized civilization in the Indus Valley of north-western India around 3000 B.C.E. Excavations of ancient cities like Mohenjo-Daro and Harappa show organized grid-pattern streets, in which residents were apparently divided along occupational lines. Little is known for certain about the religious traditions of these cities, but they were probably primarily oriented around agriculture. Archaeologists speculate that female fertility was a central element in the early religion because they have found numerous terracotta images of women with wide hips and elaborate headdresses. The poses of figures on some small clay seals may also indicate the presence of an early *yoga* practice involving sitting in cross-legged meditation postures. Furthermore, the cities had large centralized water tanks, which may presage the reverence for sacred rivers and ritual bathing in later Indian religions.

Around 1500 B.C.E., semi-nomadic warrior tribes called Aryans, "nobles," migrated out of Central Asia and started to arrive in India. These people, with their pastoral herding culture, were related to the tribes then migrating into Europe and thus were a part of the Indo-European language family. The Aryans contributed a number of cultural characteristics to the development of Indian civilization. They brought the Sanskrit language that would later become the classical language of India; a tripartite social system that divided people into categories of priests, warriors, and food-producers and would later form the ideological basis for the caste system; an elaborate ritual practice of sacrifice on fire altars; and worship of a pantheon of deities. Most of these gods and goddesses were embodiments of natural or cultural forces, that is, deities of sun, fire, earth, dawn, speech, thunderstorm, wisdom, etc. The deities were praised in hymns which were recorded in the oldest religious texts of India, called the Vedas. The Vedas also include descriptions of the sacrificial ritual and the songs to be sung in accompaniment to rituals. Later texts added commentaries to explain the meanings and consequences of the rites.

The sacrificial ritual was the center of religious life in ancient India, and the hereditary priesthood, which was made up of members of the *brahmin* social class, achieved great power and authority because of their role in the sacrificial rites. Through the performance of these rituals, it was believed, they ensured the prosperity of kingdoms and the very balance and security of creation itself. However, a growing number of religious sages began to criticize the emphasis on ritual and argued that practices without understanding were meaningless. They set in motion a new quest for knowledge, especially about the nature of the cosmos. Their intuitions and speculations about the ultimate principle underlying creation are recorded in a set of texts called the Upanishads. After suggesting such primary essences as food, water, and breath, the sages developed a beautifully subtle theory about the underlying principle of the universe as an indefinable, unknowable "something," which they called Brahman.

At the same time, they also speculated about the true nature of humanity. What part of the person is the true self? they asked themselves. What aspect defines the individual? What or who is it that says, "This body is *mine*"? What part of the individual is not subject to the vicissitudes of bodily life, and (since it is not defined by the mortal body) lives on after the body falls away? These questions led to the idea of an inner essence of the self called the *atman*. The *atman* was defined as the unique identifying aspect of the individual, and it was characterized as changeless and immortal. These attributes were also the characteristic attributes of the Brahman, the underlying principle of the cosmos, and thus the two came to be identified. For the Upanishadic sages, the highest knowledge was the realization of the identity of the individual *atman* and the universal Brahman. Personal achievement of this knowledge became the goal of religious seekers. Some took up ascetic practices to gain control of their bodies and minds in their quest for higher knowledge, while others chose a path of study to try to pierce the veils of ignorance and misconception that prevented them from seeing beyond material forms. Hermits and communities of seekers followed these new paths and formed schools with particular teachings and yogic meditation practices. From 900 to 500 B.C.E., pursuit of personal intuition about the nature of the self and the universe inspired numerous alternatives to the traditional priestly cult of fire-sacrifice.

In the sixth century B.C.E., another religious force arose that gradually displaced the priestly sacrificial tradition in the courts of India's rulers. A young noble named Siddhartha left the sheltered life of his palace on a quest for knowledge that would free him from the human torments of sickness, old age, and death. After years of following different ascetic paths and studying with various scholars, Siddhartha abandoned all these seemingly useless practices and sat down under a tree to meditate until the knowledge he sought was revealed to him or he died in the attempt. And there, under the Bodhi tree (the "awakening" tree), he finally reached the knowledge he sought. Siddhartha realized that all human suffering was the result of our attachments to things in our lives, things which are, by their own natures, impermanent and changing, but which we always wish to remain static and unchanging. Thus, life must always involve suffering as long as we are attached to transient things and plagued with desires for unattainable permanence. With this new perception, young Siddhartha became free from all attachments and became the Buddha, the "enlightened one." He then set out to teach other people a path to liberation designed to bring them to the same realization that he had found. The Buddha travelled around India, preaching about freedom from suffering for all people through personal effort and without priestly ritual. Buddhism spread rapidly, especially when it received royal sponsorship from King Ashoka (ca. 269–232 B.C.E.), who ruled over a large kingdom in India called the Mauryan Empire.

One of the Buddha's contemporaries, Vardhamana Mahavira, founded another religious tradition that spread through northern and central India and is still extant today. This tradition came to be called Jainism because its great teachers are *jina*s, "conquerors," who show others the path of salvation. For Jains, the world is full of living entities that are present in people, animals, plants, and even rocks. Salvation requires avoiding evil conduct, especially the infliction of harm on others. To avoid causing harm to these living entities, Jains developed an elaborate code of behavior. Monks sweep the ground in front of them as they walk to avoid stepping on any small beings, and wear filters over their faces so they won't accidentally inhale and harm any insects or micro-organisms. Although an ascetic monastic life is really the only way to carry out Jain precepts, layfolk are also encouraged to practice *ahimsa*, "not causing harm," as much as possible. Thus, Jain laity work primarily in commerce and trade because farming and animal husbandry would require them to kill plants and animals. Despite the rigorousness of its ethical code, Jainism attracted adherents from the wealthiest classes of society, who built beautiful temples that housed images of perfected saints as inspiration for others. The tradition has maintained a fairly steady membership throughout the centuries.

Although Buddhism remained the major religion of the ruling classes in India until the second century C.E., popular traditions of devotion to specific deities were gaining prominence among the people at the village level. Gradually, the *brahmin* priests began to make a comeback after adapting their ritual practices to these popular devotional traditions. This new combination can be seen in the great epics, the *Mahabharata* (which includes the *Bhagavadgita*) and the *Ramayana*, both of which were compiled from approximately 200 B.C.E. to 200 C.E. The following period, from 320 to 500 C.E., called the Gupta period, is considered the classical age of Indian culture and religion. The ideological social hierarchy that placed priests at the top, followed by nobility, merchants and artisans, and peasants at the bottom, became a reality in this era. During this period, the old pantheon of deities was reinterpreted in accord with a new belief in a single, supreme deity with many different forms and attributes. Three figures emerged as the central images for the supreme deity in Indian religion: Shiva, Vishnu, and Devi (the Goddess). Each of these was described as the one true God by his or her respective devotees. Thus a follower of Shiva would say that Shiva was the highest god, and all the other gods were merely forms he had taken to fulfill various functions or reveal specific teachings, while a devotee of Devi or Vishnu would describe the same pattern but grant the supreme position to his or her chosen deity.

The three great deities (Shiva, Vishnu, and Devi) were worshiped in elaborate temples built under the direct guidance of the priests. The *brahmin* priest had to formally install the image in the temple. Rituals were performed every morning and evening, as well as during the yearly festivals and for special occasions such as the need for rain in times of drought or at the beginning of a war. The core ritual, called *puja*, involved offerings made to the image. Householders could perform a similar *puja* ritual at home for the household deities.

The Gupta period also saw a great expansion of philosophical literature and the formation of elaborate mythologies which came to be recorded in texts called the Puranas. These texts focused on how to attain higher knowledge and, hence, liberation from the cycle of rebirths; yogic exercises to control the body and mind; meritorious works; the correct performance of rituals; and detailed accounts of the deeds of the gods, in which diverse mythological traditions were united to form coherent narratives. The Puranas also began to emphasize the efficacy of *bhakti*, "devotion to God," as an essential element in religion. The emotional impetus of devotion and the desire to become aware of the presence of God was supposed to inspire the seeker to live a life in accord with good works, to be continuously focused on the divine element of the material world, and to overcome any base temptations that might separate him or her from God.

Devotional elements became part of most of the Indian religions. The *bhakti* (devotional) philosophy can most easily be described through the example of Krishna worship. Krishna is said to be an incarnation of the great god Vishnu, who took human birth in the world for the sake of his followers. We are living in the Kali Age, the dark age of the world, and Krishna came to teach people about the path of devotion, which is the religious practice best suited to life in this time. The stories that depict Krishna as a young, dark-skinned cowherd who danced and played his flute in the forest with the adoring milkmaids are beloved by all Hindus to this day. These tales are used as an example of the proper attitude for a devotee, whose life should be like those of the milkmaids. The devotee of God is consumed by an ecstatic longing for God that supersedes all other considerations. Singing songs of devotion, meditating, and worshiping God's image are all ways for the seeker to reach an intuitive, immediate experience of God's all-pervasive presence.

The devotional path did not, however, displace the practices centered around yogic meditation and ritual; rather, all these existed side by side and were intermingled in day-to-day religion. The priests performed rituals before the images in temples and devotees meditated on their chosen deities. It is at this point, in the Gupta period, that Hinduism took on its classical form. Hinduism is thus a blend of ritual, meditation, and popular devotion shaped by the priestly, sacrificial tradition, and also incorporates influences from the monastic, anti-priestly traditions of Buddhism and Jainism. At the same time, the changes that took place within the Hindu tradition were mirrored in the other religions of India. Buddhism, which began by insisting on the humanity of the Buddha, evolved a new school called Mahayana Buddhism, which taught the idea of an eternal, supreme Buddha who could help his devotees achieve enlightenment. Jains and Buddhists both set up images of their teachers in their temples, much as the Hindus set up the images of deities, although there has been a fairly consistent effort to teach that the images of the Buddha and Jinas are only a reminder of the efficacy of the path, not objects of worship.

Early on, the religions of India were carried beyond the boundaries of the Indian sub-continent. Buddhism became the dominant religion of Sri Lanka, the island to the south of India, as early as the second century B.C.E. Mahayana Buddhism moved northeast into China. A later school of Buddhism that emerged out of Mahayana became popular in Tibet and the Himalayan region in the eighth century C.E. Both Buddhism and Hinduism traveled into Southeast Asia, becoming part of the traditions of Burma, Thailand, and Indonesia. As these religions spread, they carried Indian ideas about social structure, the nature of the cosmos, the natures of humanity and divinity, the goals of human life, and the means of achieving those goals. It is important therefore to understand some of the core ideas that affect religion and society across South Asia despite the number of different religions and the diversity of regional practices within traditions.

Themes of the South Asian Worldview

Caste

Perhaps the first thing that comes to mind for most people in relation to Indian society is the caste system. Caste refers to the division of society into a hierarchy of social levels determined by birth and occupation. There are actually two interlaced social hierarchies in India, the four-tiered caste system described earlier as a legacy of the Aryans, and a much more complicated organization based on family and occupational relations. The basic Indian caste hierarchy laid out in the scriptures divides people into four groups that are ranked in descending order of status: (1) priests, (2) nobility, (3) merchants and artisans, and (4) peasants and laborers. There is also a fifth group of "untouchables," who are outside the system and are employed in "unclean" occupations such as leather-working, funerary duties, and sanitation. Traditionally, members of this lowest level of society have been excluded from temples and relegated to separate areas of towns, because their presence was thought to be polluting to people and places. This hierarchy is based on an idea of purity in relation to religion, rather than wealth or power in society. Today, the Indian government has outlawed the exclusion of "untouchables" from public and religious facilities and is working to provide opportunities for economic improvement to those once relegated to the lowest ranks.

The second caste system is called *jati* or *jajmani*, which literally means "birth." The system is based primarily on family ties and occupational groupings. At the village level in rural India, certain families are associated with certain occupations. There are groups of weavers, goldsmiths, oil pressers, launderers, barbers, and so forth, and all these family occupations are passed on from father to son. Each occupation has a different status in relation to other occupations, although the hierarchical rankings of these groups vary from village to village and may change over time as one *jati* gains or loses wealth and social prestige. The *jajmani* system, as it is often called, is important because a member of one *jati* must marry a member of the same group and, since there are additional rules in north India prohibiting marriage to someone from the same village or from a family that is too closely related to one's own, matches must be made with members of the same *jati* in a distant village. To further complicate matters, there are sub-groups within the various *jatis*.

Above and beyond the more well-known four-tiered caste hierarchy, it is this amazingly complicated system of *jatis* which affects the lives of most Indians. The rankings are, however, breaking down in modern urban centers, where people are moving out of their traditional family occupations and are mixing on more equalized social levels in education and at work. Today it is primarily in matters of marital eligibility that *jati* still plays a major role.

While most of the non-Hindu religions in South Asia, such as Buddhism, Islam, and Christianity, claim to reject the caste hierarchies, the systems still affect them. Converts to non-Hindu traditions may be drawn from particular castes and may replicate *jati*-based marital patterns even after conversion. Historically, although newly founded religious groups may reject caste divisions, especially those based on the four-tiered pattern which sets priests up as intermediaries between God and devotee, over time most religious groups develop their own internal hierarchies. Periodically, reform movements flare up and the divisions are temporarily leveled, but it is hard to eliminate an organizational principle that has shaped a society for thousands of years.

The preference for choosing marriage partners from within the boundaries defined by *jati* shows little sign of fading. This is not just a matter of convention; there are practical benefits. Parents are responsible for arranging their children's marriages, and they draw on their kinship networks to find eligible spouses. Choosing a son- or daughter-in-law requires information about the prospective family member's personal habits, education, earning potential, and family obligations. This information is acquired through family connections. Furthermore, by marrying within the *jati*, one is assured a spouse who shares cultural traditions like food preferences, language, and behavioral patterns, and who is already familiar with the family business.

Karma

The idea of *karma* is central to Indian religion and has also influenced non-native traditions like Islam and Christianity. The term *karma* means "action," and the theory behind the principle of *karma* is that every action causes an effect. One will eventually experience the effects of one's actions, if not in this lifetime, then in those to come. Belief in *karma* makes it possible to explain life events. If something bad happens to a good person, it is because he or she is experiencing the result of actions in previous lives. Although some Westerners have criticized the doctrine of *karma* as leading to a sense of fatalism, most Indians see it as providing a powerful way to understand and accept the things that life brings. If troubles occur in one's own life, the usual attitude is a sense of relief that the negative karmic debts of past lives are now being discharged, so one is being freed from the burden of those old debts.

Cycle of Rebirth

The idea of *karma* is directly linked to the idea of *samsara*, the cycle of rebirth. According to this belief, one is continually reborn into the world in order to experience the consequences of one's actions in previous lives. Theoretically, if one lives a meritorious life, one may be reborn as a god and live a life of pleasure in heaven until the merit is used up, then return to earthly life once again. In the same way, one may be reborn as an animal if one has been guilty of serious crimes. To be born on earth as a human being is seen as a great opportunity, since only people can work to break out of the cycle of rebirth. Animals do not possess the right intelligence and abilities, while those who sport in the celestial realms are too happy to realize that they should be seeking a permanent solution to their transient existence. Only in our world of mixed pleasure and pain is liberation possible. The goal of religion, therefore, is to break the cycle of rebirth by learning to live in such a way as not to incur any karmic debt. This requires freeing oneself from attachment to worldly success and possessions, so that one can perform the actions of daily life without desiring the results of those actions. When one finally achieves a state in which one is no longer attached to the fruits of one's actions, one no longer builds up karmic debt, and thus actions no longer lead to the necessity of rebirth.

This idea of cyclic lives is used to describe the cyclic existence of the cosmos itself. The entire universe, it is believed, is periodically destroyed and re-created in an endless cycle. Creation goes through a set pattern of progressive ages, each more degraded than the former. The various Indian religions have distinct cosmological systems, but, in general, all agree that the current age is marked by a mixture of pain and joy, and that it is this blend of suffering and happiness that spurs people to seek something better.

The Ultimate Goal of Religion

The ultimate goal of religion in South Asia, stated most simply, is to break out of *samsara*, the cycle of birth and rebirth. Descriptions of what happens when that cycle is broken differ among traditions. The Hindu devotee, for example, seeks eternity in the divine realm of a personal God. The Hindu *yogi* (ascetic) who meditates on God as the impersonal Absolute (or Brahman) seeks dissolution in the formless unity of that Supreme Brahman. For his part, the Buddhist seeks *nirvana*, a state of complete calm marked by the "blowing out" of desire, while the Jain purifies his soul of the material *karma* that weighs it down so that it can float free and rise to the top of the cosmos. All of these visions of the final, blissful existence are different, but they all are seen as the result of the cessation of the cycle of rebirth.

The Nature of the Material World

The religions of South Asia do not separate the transcendent from the immanent as radically as do Western religions. In those Hindu traditions that posit a creator, the deity is both the active and the material cause of all existence. God pervades his creation, yet the cosmos is not the entirety of God. All creation is the embodiment of a mere fragment of the Supreme Being. For traditions that do not believe in a creator deity, like Buddhism, there is still a belief in the underlying unified nature of everything that exists. This oneness, however, is on the subtle level, and lies beyond the perceptions of the senses, which only register the surface diversity. The perceived material world with all its diversity is described as *maya*, an "illusion," because it is not really diverse at all when one becomes aware that on a subtle level everything is ultimately the same. Indeed, it is this conception of the subtle nature underlying both the material world and the transcendent world that forms the basis for the religious practices of South Asia. One of the goals of religion is to realize the true nature of one's own self with respect to this subtle nature. To do this requires training the body and mind in order to achieve knowledge beyond that which can be received through the physical senses. For religious elites, physical discipline, study, and meditation are the key practices for achieving this knowledge, while the devotional worship, chanting, and dancing found in popular sects serve the same role for householders by focusing the body and mind on the transcendent.

The Medieval and Modern Periods

The core ideas described above shaped all the Indian religions, but the specific practices and beliefs of South Asians vary considerably from region to region. India alone has sixteen major literary languages, each spoken in a particular geographical area with its own distinct cultural habits, and the Himalayan area represents yet another linguistic-cultural complex. Every one of these areas has its own religious traditions oriented around local deities and myths. From the Gupta period (320–500 C.E.) on, wandering monks and religious teachers have carried devotional songs and religious teachings focused on devotion to particular deities from one region to another, where they have then been adapted by local holy men and women. Particularly gifted poet-saints often became the centers of circles of followers who established small religious sects based on their ecstatic songs. *Gurus*, that is men (and some women) who had achieved awareness of the presence of the divine in their daily lives and felt called to teach others, formulated their own systems of practices and beliefs, drawing on ideas from the Vedas, Upanishads, and popular songs of devotion as well as ascetic *yoga* techniques and traditional rituals. These regional sects are the living, ever-changing center of Hinduism. The sects proliferated, especially from the thirteenth to the eighteenth centuries, when the devotional movements multiplied and flourished.

The rise of the devotional movements helped the Indians to withstand the proselytizing of external religions, first Islam and then Christianity. In the eighteenth century, Arab Muslims conquered the Sind, a region on the northwestern edge of India. From there they started fighting their way into the north Indian plain. Inland Bengal in the northeast of India was conquered in the thirteenth century, and colonization of the interior areas was being undertaken by Muslim raiders between 1295 and 1323. Gradually the entire Indian sub-continent came under Muslim rule.

The period of Muslim dominion shaped India's modern religions. The early rulers of the Delhi Sultanate, which governed north India from 1206–1526 C.E., did not have sufficient troops to force all Indians to convert to Islam, so they designated Hinduism a "religion of the book," thereby according it legal status as a legitimate religious tradition. The pragmatic tolerance of the early rule was, however, followed by periods of conflict. Buddhism completely disappeared from India after its last monasteries were raided and destroyed by Muslims. Many of the Mughal rulers (ca. 1526–1757), of Turkish ancestry, were particularly intolerant of Indian religions. During this period, the external practices of Hinduism, which were not compatible with Islam, were attacked. Muslims did not approve of the use of images in worship, so they destroyed a tremendous amount of temple artwork. Moreover, religious leaders were periodically imprisoned, especially if there seemed to be a threat of Muslims being attracted to their teachings.

Despite this official policy, there was still great respect for holy men of both traditions among the village folk, and close ties developed between the Muslim and Hindu mystical traditions. Furthermore, Islam, with its doctrine of equality and its rejection of priestly authority, appealed to many Indians. Whole groups of Hindus converted, especially those who belonged to low-level castes. By the twentieth century, India would have the third largest Muslim population of any country in the world.

The pressure to convert to Islam during the Mughal period also stirred a reexamination of Indian religion and brought renewed life to Hinduism. Dynamic leaders from the devotional traditions appeared, and new Indian sects emerged. Some claimed to be heirs to the old Upanishadic wisdom and advocated strict adherence to brahmanical (priestly) tradition. Others rejected identification with either Hinduism or Islam, and drew on key elements of both religions to describe their faiths. Among the latter were the followers of the weaver-poet Kabir and the disciples of Guru Nanak, the founder of Sikhism. The latter tradition in particular has grown to be a religion distinct from either Hindusim or Islam, with a large following in the northwestern part of India.

The tensions between indigenous Indian traditions and those imported by foreign rule persisted during the subsequent era of British dominance, which began at the end of the eighteenth century. Fear that children would convert to Islam was now replaced by fear of Christian proselytizing. Inspired by these new cultural and religious challenges, English-educated leaders led reform movements, like the Brahmo Samaj, which sought to eliminate aspects of the old Indian traditions that now seemed problematic and outdated—practices such as the immolation of widows on their husbands' funeral pyres (*suttee*). The reformers argued that such practices were not part of the pure Hindu *dharma* and were not found in the wisdom of the Upanishads. The Brahmo Samaj movement was open to Western culture, but other reform movements, such as the Arya Samaj, founded by Swami Dayananda (1824–1883), rejected all Western traditions and upheld the superiority of the ancient Vedic tradition. The Arya Samaj movement agitated for reforms based on the Vedas, which it argued taught monotheism and morality, not worship of images or caste discrimination. Such movements helped Hindus regain a sense of the value of their traditions in spite of foreign rule. They also created a new attitude toward social practices as distinct from religious life, so that Indians began to examine which practices were part of their spiritual traditions and which were merely ordained by social-cultural conventions.

The best known of all Hindu reform movements is the Ramakrishna Mission, founded by Swami Vivekananda (1863–1902), a disciple of Paramahansa Ramakrishna (1836–1886). Vivekananda took part in the World's Parliament of Religions in Chicago in 1893, and inspired a new interest in Hinduism among Americans. The acclaim he received at the parliament brought great pride to Hindu India and set in motion a new effort to spread Hinduism to the West. Vivekananda also brought back to India a sense of the need to improve social conditions, for which purpose he established relief organizations, schools, hospitals, etc. To carry out these activities, he organized the Ramakrishna Mission, which now has centers around the world, and the Ramakrishna monastic order, which guides the activities of the centers.

Vivekananda marks the emergence of the modern voice of international Hinduism. Educated in both Western and Indian thought, Vivekananda could speak about his natal tradition in terms that were comprehensible to a Western audience. He was the first of many famous leaders in the twentieth century, leaders such as Aurobindo Ghose, Sarvepalli Radhakrishnan, and Mahatma Gandhi, who have used this cross-cultural ability to teach the world about Hinduism. In turn, these leaders, and many others, have also shaped modern Hindu thought. Forced to define their traditions in order to differentiate their faith from other religions, they have also helped their traditions adapt to the needs of a changing world.

Sri Lanka and Tibet have adapted along different lines. In Sri Lanka, the Theravada Buddhist tradition was nearly lost when British rule undermined the traditional state support of the monasteries. Strong Christian missionary efforts and mandatory Christian education as part of school curricula further weakened Buddhism. Then the tide turned when a Buddhist monk won a series of public debates about the merits of Buddhism versus Christianity, and the ordination lineage was revived by a delegation of monks from Thailand. Meanwhile, the American Theosophist Henry Olcott brought Western respect to Buddhism through his studies and writing, and the British Pali Text Society began to collect and translate the Buddhist canon. Today, Buddhism is once again firmly established as the primary religion of Sri Lanka, while the English fluency of the Sri Lankan monks makes their tradition one of the most accessible to Westerners.

The European presence in South Asia had less effect on Tibet, which had few exploitable resources and was not easily accessible. The Tibetans really began to interact with the West only after the Chinese Communist occupation caused large numbers of Tibetans to flee into India and Bhutan. Since then, Tibetan monks have studied at British universities and have spread around the world to share their Vajrayana Buddhist tradition with others.

Conclusion

This book discusses religions from South Asia—that is, the area stretching from Sri Lanka in the south up to Tibet on the northern side of the Himalayas—which are being transplanted to California. It is primarily concerned only with the indigenous South Asian religions, since the Muslim, Christian, and Jewish traditions are addressed by other volumes in the Religious Contours of California series. Chapter One has given a brief description of the history of South Asian religions and some of the core ideas that these traditions share. The next chapter looks at the experience of the Punjabi Sikhs, who formed the first sizeable South Asian community in California at the beginning of the twentieth century. The third chapter describes the more recent migration of Hindu Indians and their efforts to establish religious centers and temples complete with traditional images of deities brought over from India. Chapter Four deals with two distinct Buddhist traditions coming from Asia, the Theravada Buddhism of Sri Lanka, Burma, and Thailand, and the Vajrayana Buddhism of Tibet. Finally, Chapter Five examines American approaches to South Asian religious traditions, from the early interest in Oriental philosophy and mysticism to a growing appreciation for the richness of the worldview and lifestyle that forms the context for these religious ideologies and practices.

2 Sikhs: The Khalsa in California

In 1912, a group of South Asians from the Punjab region of north-western India formed an organization called the Pacific Coast Khalsa Diwan Society and purchased a piece of property in Stockton, California, as a site for the first Sikh *gurdwara* (temple) in the United States. The land had a house on it that served temporarily as a *gurdwara*, but the congregation outgrew it almost immediately, so a new building was constructed by 1916. As the first East Indian religious center in California, it became a gathering place for South Asians of all faiths. Muslims and Hindus met there to socialize and were allowed to observe their own religious practices as long as these did not violate the behavioral etiquette of the Sikh house of worship. Since Sikhism was the faith of the majority of the South Asians in the Golden State before 1965 and was the first tradition to establish a religious center in California, it seems natural to begin a history of South Asian religions in California with this tradition.

History of Sikhism

The *gurdwara* is both a communal and a religious center for the Sikhs. It houses the sacred scripture that holds the teachings of the Sikh religion and is the locus for festivals and for the performance of life rituals, such as marriage. At the same time, the *gurdwara* is a place to affirm the unity of the Sikh community as a socio-political group. For Sikhism is a religious faith associated with a particular community of people with a shared history and culture, who have come to see themselves as a coherent socio-cultural unit. The dual identity of the Sikhs, as a religious and a cultural body, is symbolized by the two swords that grace the flag flying over the *gurdwara*. These swords, reminders of a Sikh *guru* (teacher) who took up arms to defend his people against the oppression of India's Muslim rulers, are said to represent the *guru*'s role as both *piri*, "religious leader," and *miri*, "political leader." The Sikhs have looked to their own leaders for temporal as well as spiritual guidance. This dual emphasis within the tradition reflects the historical struggle of the Sikhs.

The Sikh tradition developed in the Punjab area of northwestern India in the early sixteenth century, a region that had been invaded by Muslim conquerors and suffered years of conflict and bloodshed. In the midst of this chaos, a man who came to be known as Guru Nanak (1469–1539) had a vision of God's presence and was given the command to go out into the world and teach a new path focused on repetition of God's name, the practice of charity, service, meditation, and worship. This was the beginning of Sikhism.

Guru Nanak rejected the claims of religious primacy put forward by both the Hindus and Muslims, teaching that true religion was beyond the empty rituals and narrow dogmas of either tradition. With the proclamation, "There is no Hindu and no Muslim," Guru Nanak established a new tradition that drew on aspects of both Hinduism and Islam. He taught belief in a single creator God, like the Muslim Allah, but he designated this God Satnam (True Name) instead of using the Muslim title of Allah or any of the sectarian Hindu names, like Vishnu or Shiva. Nanak's worldview was basically Indian; he retained Hindu ideas about *karma*, reincarnation, and *maya*, the ultimate unreality of the world. He believed that the highest goal of human life was to seek communion with God, and he emphasized the importance of the *guru* as the teacher who leads people to this goal.

Guru Nanak journeyed to the major religious centers of South Asia, sharing his message with others. Stories of his travels describe him rebuking Muslim and Hindu authorities for performing rituals without true devotion, ridiculing social hierarchies like the caste system as meaningless (because true purity depends on moral character, not social class or occupation), and teaching that true religion requires devotion to God and a life of service. In 1521, Nanak settled in Kartarpur with his family, and a community of followers grew up around him. Here he built a home, a hostel for vistors, and a place for teaching that was the precursor of the modern *gurdwara*. He lived the life of a householder, not a monk, setting an example for his followers of how to carry out his teachings in daily life. He rejected popular Hindu practices like ancestor worship, astrology, and rituals in which a priest serves as an intermediary between people and God and advocated the use of meditation and singing of his own devotional hymns.

In September 1539, Guru Nanak initiated a follower named Lehna (sometimes called Lahina) as his successor and gave him the new name of Guru Angad, which means "limb of the *guru*." During this ceremony, Guru Nanak gave Angad a book of his own hymns, thereby entrusting him with the divine message that God had given to him. Later, Sikhs came to understand that all the *guru*s in this lineage are bearers of this same message, so that even though the teacher changed, the teaching remained the same. The Sikh chronicler Bhai Gurdas gave this description:

> Before he [Guru Nanak] died he installed Lehna and set the Guru's canopy over his head. Merging his light in Guru Angad's light the Sat Guru changed his form. None could comprehend this, he revealed a wonder of wonders, changing his body he made Guru Angad's body his own. (Var I, pauri 45)

Twenty-one days later, Guru Nanak died, but the fledgling faith he left behind continued to grow and mature into the Sikh religion. At the core of Sikhism are Nanak's teachings, preserved in his hymns. The practices of the Sikhs are based on Nanak's instructions to his followers to live a householder's life, to regard work as a form of divine service, to sing devotional songs, and to meditate on the divine name. These instructions were preserved and elaborated by the *guru*s who succeeded Nanak and continued to teach according to the divine message of the first *guru*.

Nanak was the first in a series of ten Sikh *guru*s, teachers who combined the roles of religious and community leadership. Each was regarded as the human speaker of the Word of God, and as such had the authority to adapt the Sikh teachings to the changes that history brought to the Punjab. The first four *guru*s lived in fairly peaceful times. Although India was ruled by the Mughals, Muslims of Turkish ancestry, this period coincided with the reign of Akbar (1556–1605), the most religiously tolerant of all the Mughal emperors. Because of this, the *guru*s were able to focus on organizing the growing religious tradition. They distributed copies of Guru Nanak's hymns to the growing number of Sikh congregations and organized their followers into regional groups. The *guru*s worked on behalf of their people, asking the Mughal emperor to lighten their tax burdens during hard times and to repeal taxes on pilgrims visiting holy sites. They institutionalized the practice of Guru Ka Langar, the "*guru*'s kitchen," that had begun with Guru Nanak. All who came to meet the *guru* were required to gather together for a meal, thereby emphasizing the unity and equality of all, regardless of caste, social status, or religious affiliation. The third *guru*, Amar Das, required Sikhs to gather at his teaching center for special celebrations during the Hindu spring and autumn festivals of Baisakhi (New Year's) and Divali (Feast of Lights) so they would have to consciously choose one religion or the other. The fourth *guru*, Ram Das, began the construction of the first temple at Amritsar, which is today the site of the newly rebuilt Golden Temple and the headquarters of the world Sikh community. The original temple was completed under the fifth *guru*, Arjan, who also installed within it the *Guru Granth Sahib* (also known as the *Adi Granth*), the collected writings of the Sikh *guru*s and several poet-saints. Amritsar became a pilgrimage center and is the most holy city for Sikhs today.

In 1605, the religiously tolerant Mughal ruler Akbar died, and the peaceful relations between Sikhs and their Muslim rulers came to an end. Guru Arjan became the first Sikh martyr when he was executed, allegedly for supporting a contender to the Mughal throne. His son, Guru Hargobind, took up arms and began to form a militia. From this time on, Sikhs began to speak of the need for both spiritual and temporal authority for their community. The next four *guru*s were faced with troubled times in which brief periods of peace were interspersed with prolonged stretches of intense conflict. For a time, the Sikhs were reduced to a remnant living on horseback as guerilla forces in the Punjab. The ninth *guru* was named Tegh Bahadur, "brave sword," for his courage in battles against Mughal forces. He was executed when he refused to convert to Islam.

The tenth *guru*, Gobind Singh (1666–1708), reorganized the Sikh community to meet the exigencies of this era of struggle and, in the process, gave the Sikh community many of the distinctive aspects by which it is known today. In 1699, at Baisakhi, the New Year's Festival gathering, Gobind Singh formed the Khalsa, or the Community of the Pure, to which all Sikhs, both male and female, could belong. Members were initiated by means of a ritual in which they drank and were sprinkled with sweetened water that had been stirred with a sword. Initiated men then took the name Singh (lion) and women took the name Kaur (princess) to emphasize the unity and equality of the members of the Khalsa. Guru Gobind Singh proclaimed a code of discipline for the initiates: tobacco, eating animals slaughtered according to Muslim ritual, and sexual relations with Muslims were prohibited. Members of the Sikh community were also to avoid rival religious leaders, and the men were required to wear five symbols, known collectively as the five Ks: (1) *kesh,* unshorn hair on the face and head, usually covered by a turban, signifying saintliness; (2) *kangh,* a comb for keeping the hair neat; (3) *kach,* short pants for quick movement in battle; (4) *kara,* a steel bracelet signifying sternness and restraint; (5) *kirpan,* a sword of defense. This reorganization effort brought the military forces of the Sikhs into a united body oriented toward the defence of the faith under the command of the *guru.*

Guru Gobind Singh was the last living *guru.* All four of his sons predeceased him, so when he lay dying from the wound inflicted by an assassin's knife he installed the *Adi Granth,* the book containing the collected writings of the teachers revered by the Sikhs, as the next *guru.* He renamed the book the *Guru Granth Sahib.* He told the Khalsa that the spirit of the Guru (God) was present in the word of the *gurus* as written in the *Adi Granth.* Furthermore, the spirit of the Guru was also present whenever members of the Khalsa deliberated on matters in the presence of the book, so the community would be able to guide itself. Guru Gobind Singh saw the Khalsa, the fellowship of Sikhs who lived in accord with the message of the *gurus* as this message was taught in their sacred text, as the embodiment of God.

The eighteenth century brought almost continual conflict between Sikhs and their Mughal overlords until Maharaja Ranjit Singh succeeded in establishing a Sikh state in the Punjab. This kingdom lasted from 1799 to 1849, when Maharaja Dalip Singh handed it over to the British after a series of bloody wars. During the previous reign of Ranjit Singh, the Sikh military had been upgraded to match the organization and efficiency of the British forces. The Sikhs continued to serve in the armed forces under British rule and gained reputations as excellent soldiers.

In the late nineteenth century, Sikh revival movements developed in the Punjab in reaction to both the proselytizing of Christian missionaries and the Arya Samaj Hindu reform movement. The Singh Sabha (Singh Society), which had been founded in Amritsar in 1873, expanded its work to other cities. It focused on literary and educational activities (such as setting up Sikh colleges) to revive Sikhism. There was also a push to regain control of Sikh holy sites that had come under Hindu administration.

The Sikhs, who had fought so hard against foreign rule since the seventeenth century, were also very active in the struggle for Indian independence from Britain in the twentieth century. Unfortunately, when that independence was achieved in 1947, the Punjab region, where most of the Sikhs lived, was devastated because the dividing line between India and the newly formed Muslim nation of Pakistan sliced right through it. More than two million Sikhs were forced to leave the western region and a similar number of Muslims emigrated from the east. There was considerable chaos and bloodshed, all of which has left a sense of enmity on both sides of the border. Today, the boundaries of the state of the Punjab in India are drawn to encompass the areas in which the Punjabi language is spoken, and 85 percent of the Sikhs in India live in this state. There is also a large international Sikh community made up of people seeking economic opportunites all around the world.

The relationship between the Sikhs and the Indian government has not run smoothly. Conflicts dating back to negotiations at the time of independence (1947) involve religious, economic, and cultural matters. In the 1970s and 1980s, Sikh opposition to the government of India was led by Jarnail Singh Brindranwale, who used the Golden Temple as a headquarters for his supporters. His protests sparked a period of unrest in which several hundred people were killed in the Punjab. Prime Minister Indira Gandhi ordered the Indian army to restore order and remove the opposition force from the Golden Temple. In 1984, the army attacked the temple, killing hundreds of Sikhs, and then it moved through the Punjab to quell armed resistence. Shortly thereafter, Indira Gandhi was assassinated by her Sikh bodyguards, an act which triggered riots and violence against Sikhs in cities across India. In the aftermath of this violence, the international Sikh community drew closer together. A renewed sense of identity as members of a minority, clearly distinguished from Indians or Hindus, has inspired a greater emphasis on observance of the rules of behavior laid out by the *gurus*, especially the wearing of the five Ks. There is also a political faction that is actively campaigning for an independent Sikh state, to be called Khalistan. Ironically, the Khalistan movement has created a deep division among the Sikhs, even though the traumas that inspired it have brought a greater sense of communal identity. Many Sikhs do not want to mix politics with religion. These divisions are evident in *gurdwara*s all around the world as temple governing bodies push political agendas and are met by resistance from community members who prefer to see in Sikhism a religious and cultural identity rather than a potential nationality. Today, Sikhs are struggling to balance their religion's dual emphases on spiritual and temporal authority in the modern world.

Sikh Belief and Practice

Sikhs refer to their faith as *gurmat*, "the path of the *guru*." The teachings of Guru Nanak and his successors are at the heart of the tradition. Nanak rejected asceticism in favor of *grihastha dharma*, the religion of the householder, strongly emphasizing service in this world and the importance of membership in a community focused on a life oriented towards God. The center of worship for this community is the *gurdwara*, "gateway of the *guru*." Technically, a *gurdwara* is any place where one finds an appropriately honored copy of the *Guru Granth Sahib*, the scriptural record of the *gurus*' teachings, whether it be a simple room in a family home, or a richly decorated formal temple. The activities at the *gurdwara* focus on readings from the *Guru Granth Sahib*. Each community *gurdwara* has a kitchen and dining area where all who attend services may join together in a communal meal. The *gurdwara* is also the setting for major festivals throughout the year, and for the performance of weddings, initiations, and funerals.

Guru

The *gurus* were ten human teachers who taught the message of God as it had been revealed to Guru Nanak in a mystical experience. All of the *gurus* embodied the same message, thus all were described as bearers of the same divine light. It is this divine light in the form of the *gurbani*, the "Word of God," that the Sikhs revere, not the human messenger. The real Guru, therefore, is God, and the human *gurus* were merely vehicles for God's divine instruction. The convinction that all the ten teachers were bearers of the same light is made clear in the text of the *Guru Granth Sahib*, where the *gurus* all signed their writings with the name Nanak. In the *Rehat Maryada*, the guide to the Sikh way of life formulated in 1945, it is stated that Sikhs "should believe in the unity of the Ten Gurus, that is that a single soul existed in the bodies of the Ten Gurus."

The ten *gurus* and their years of leadership are:

THE TEN GURUS	LEADERSHIP
Guru Nanak	1469–1539
Guru Angad	1539–1552
Guru Amar Das	1552–1574
Guru Ram Das	1574–1581
Guru Arjan	1581–1606
Guru Hargobind	1606–1644

Guru Har Rai	1644–1661
Guru Har Krishan	1661–1664
Guru Tegh Bahadur	1664–1675
Guru Gobind Singh	1675–1708

Since the true religious leadership lay in God's message, not the messenger, it was possible for Guru Gobind Singh to make the text that preserves the divine words into the primary religious authority for the Khalsa, the Sikh community. Individual Sikhs open the sacred text and read from it to gain advice in times of trouble, and the whole Sikh Khalsa takes guidance from the text to solve community problems. Thus the *Guru Granth Sahib* guides the community just as the human *gurus* once did. Moreover, the Khalsa itself is also considered an embodiment of the Guru. When the community gathers and turns its thoughts toward God, it too has the ability to make decisions that clarify and support the principles of faith.

God

Guru Nanak taught that there was only one God, a god who created and pervades everything. God is formless and, being eternal and transcendent, could never have taken human birth as an incarnation like Krishna. Thus, Sikhism rejects the Hindu idea of divine incarnations, worship of images, and temple rituals. Since God pervades everything, distinctions of caste, gender differentiation, and concepts of purity and pollution are also considered false because such distinctions suggest that God has greater or lesser presence in some things than in others. Nanak enforced this rejection of social distinctions by establishing a communal meal (*langar* or *pangat*) where everyone ate together—a blatant violation of caste practices. When Guru Gobind Singh required all members of the Khalsa to take the same last name, he further eliminated caste divisions from the Sikh community.

In the Sikh tradition, the pervasiveness of God is often illustrated by a story about Nanak's journey to Mecca. While traveling to the Holy City, the *guru* fell asleep with his feet pointing toward Mecca. An outraged Muslim awoke him and chastised him for the disrespectful action of pointing his impure feet toward God. Nanak calmly requested the Muslim to turn his feet toward some direction where God did not exist. In a more philosophical vein, Sikhism also defines God as *sat*, which means both "truth" and "reality," as opposed to *asat*, "falsehood" and "illusion." This implies that God, the formless impersonal Absolute, not only pervades all creation, but is present in virtuous behavior as well. If God is truth, then to speak a falshood is to be ungodly. A good Sikh should, therefore, avoid ungodly behavior such as lying, cheating, adultery, etc. because such activities carry one away from the presence of God.

Worship

Sikh practices strive to bring an awareness of how to live in conformity with God's truth in daily life. In the *Rehat Maryada*, a written guide to the Sikh way of life, Sikhs are instructed to rise early, bathe, and then meditate on the one true God. Next, they should recite a series of prayers, beginning with the Japji, a prayer that was composed by Guru Nanak. In those families which strictly observe these devotions, the prayers will usually be followed by a reading from the *Guru Granth Sahib*. To do so, the head of the household will remove the night covering from the text, open it at random, and read aloud the first hymn on the left-hand page. This passage then becomes a focus for contemplation throughout the day. If a Sikh does not have a copy of the *Granth* at home, he or she may go to the community *gurdwara* and draw a passage from the text there. Finally, in the evening, two other formal prayers are recited.

The *Guru Granth Sahib* is the focus of both private worship and communal services. At the Golden Temple in Punjab, for example, a commandment from the text is selected every morning and written on a chalkboard for all to see. Hymns from the text are recited at large gatherings, and Sikhs are supposed to contemplate their meanings so as to make them applicable to daily life. In addition, all Sikhs are encouraged to learn the *gurmukhi* script so that they can read a lesson from the text themselves without relying on others, and they are encouraged to periodically read the text from beginning to end. Special occasions may be accompanied by an *akhand path*, a ritual in which the whole text is read straight through by a relay of readers. Such readings take about forty-eight hours to complete.

Reading and contemplating the *Guru Granth Sahib* is not the only practice of Sikhism. Guru Nanak also advocated keeping company with those who live according to religious precepts (*sangat*), listening to and singing devotional hymns (*kirtan*), and engaging in meditation on the presence of God (*nam simran*). Such activities may be part of everyday practice or form a part of the communal ceremonies performed on special occasions.

Sikhism provides a comprehensive description of how to live life according to religion (*dharma*). Sikhs should avoid non-Sikh religious practices, such as reverence for images of God, and they should live a life based on the *gurus'* teachings. Such a life includes: rejecting ideas about caste, pollution, and astrology; educating one's children in the Sikh faith; avoiding alcohol, drugs, and tobacco; earning an honest living; giving to charity; avoiding gambling and theft; respecting all women as if they were members of one's own family; and being faithful to one's spouse.

Anyone who lives by the precepts of Sikhism is considered a member of the Khalsa. Such a person is qualified to lead services at the *gurdwara*, for there are no special priests in the community. Some people are specially trained in the reading of the *Guru Granth Sahib*, and a Sikh community may employ such a person as a *granthi*, a person who leads readings, cares for the text, and often serves as custodian of the *gurdwara*. Ideally, however, all the members of the Khalsa are capable of performing the public readings. The reader (the *granthi*), or a respected scholar who visits a *gurdwara*, may give a discourse on the text as part of a service, but all talks must be based on the teachings of the *gurus*, and care is taken not to contradict the tenets of the tradition.

Nam Simran

The goal of religious practice in Sikhism is to direct one's whole life to God's service. In this way, one becomes *gurmukh*, "God-oriented," instead of being focused on a self-reliant (*manmukh*) quest for personal material gain. In general, therefore, a Sikh should keep God's name continually in mind, earn a living by honest means, and give to charity. Specifically, however, *nam simran* is the practice which leads the Sikh to the goal of immediate union with God. Nam literally means "name," but in the writings of the *gurus* it can better be interpreted as the manifest aspect of God which extends throughout all creation and gives form to everything. It is called the creator and the supporter of the whole universe, and it represents God manifest and immanently active in the universe. An unenlightened person, self-centered and ignorant of the all-pervasive Nam, continues to think of God as separate from creation. Such a person is, therefore, bound up in the cycle of rebirth (*samsara*) and will continue to be born and to die. Through the religious teachings of the *gurus*, God reaches out to awaken people to awareness of the presence of Nam. This awareness is more than simple knowledge of a name or a transitory intuition that the individual is one with God. To become truly God-centered requires daily discipline, which is known as *nam simran*, "meditation on God's Nam."

This meditative discipline begins early for Sikhs. First, as a child, one learns the word *"waheguru,"* which originally meant "hail Guru" (God), but has become the formal designation for God, now usually translated "Wonderful Lord." Later these words become the focus of one's meditations, both in the quiet of the predawn hours and as a refrain to be repeated throughout the day. This repetition helps draw one's thoughts to God so that one can remember to live in accordance with the truth. The keeping of good company (*sangat*) and participation in devotional singing (*kirtan*) also help one maintain this discipline. In addition, one should remember to contemplate the words of the *gurus*. Living thus with God constantly in mind, the Sikh attains a state of ecstasy and discretion. The devotee sees the universe as a divine creation, an emanation of God, and the five evils of lust, anger, greed, attachment, and pride are gradually conquered. Eventually, through God's grace one attains a state of bliss. This is the state of *ajapa japa*, spontaneous remembrance, in which the mind is automatically attuned to God every moment of the day. The result is a life of service to others.

Ceremonies and Festivals

The Sikh initiation ceremony, through which people become members of the Khalsa, the Community of the Pure, still follows the pattern laid down by Guru Gobind Singh. Five adult male Sikhs, representing the first five men initiated by Gobind Singh, preside over the ceremony. They prepare *amrit* (nectar) by putting crystal sugar in water and stirring it with a sword while reciting specific hymns. The candidates repeat the words "Hail to the Guru's Khalsa! Hail to the victory of the Guru!" They then kneel while a handful of the *amrit* is given to them to drink and another handful is sprinkled on their faces five times. The officiants lead the initiates in repeating the opening statement of the *Guru Granth Sahib* before giving the initiates instructions about rules of conduct for members of the Khalsa, including keeping the five Ks. Finally, the initiates are pronounced members of the *guru's* own family. The ceremony then ends with the three basic practices of Sikhism: community prayer, opening the *Granth* at random and taking a commandment from it, and the distribution of *karah parshad*, a sweet made from flour, sugar, and butter, the sharing of which symbolizes casteless equality.

Members of the Sikh community take part in several other important ceremonies during their lives. One of these is the name-giving ceremony for a new child. The birth of a child, boy or girl, is welcomed as a gift from God, and thus, when the mother is well enough, the family visits the *gurdwara* to give thanks. There they make a monetary offering, which is used to pay for the *karah parshad* given to all who come to the *gurdwara* to celebrate with them. Sometimes the family requests a complete reading of the *Granth* at the naming ceremony, with the naming taking place at the end of the reading. The child's name is chosen by opening the text at random and reading the first word on the left-hand page. The parents then choose a name beginning with the same initial and the *granthi* (the designated public reader) announces it publicly, adding Kaur for a girl and Singh for a boy. Next prayers are read and the *karah parshad* is shared with the congregation. If it is not possible to go to a *gurdwara*, the naming may also be done at home.

The most festive of all life rituals is the marriage ceremony. Marriages are usually arranged by the families. Selection of a spouse is supposed to focus first on considerations of virtuous behavior, good temperament, and appropriate age, and only take issues of social status and economic position into consideration secondarily. Caste often plays a role in marriage arrangements, but there are many exceptions to this since it is more important to marry a Sikh than to marry within one's caste. For Sikhs, therefore, the primary emphasis is on establishing a family that will be united in its adherence to their religious traditions.

The wedding normally takes place in the bride's hometown and may be celebrated in any building as long as a copy of the *Guru Granth Sahib* is present. The ceremony takes place at the morning service. After the morning hymn, the groom and bride come forward to sit at the foot of the *Granth*. Whoever is conducting the marriage leads prayers asking God to bless the couple. The couple then publicly assents to the marriage by bowing toward the *Granth*. Next the bride's scarf is tied to a cloth on the groom's shoulders and together they circumambulate the *Granth* while the congregation sings hymns. The service concludes with the prayers and the serving of *karah parshad*. This simple ceremony is usually just a small part of the wedding festivities, which may include processions, receptions with exchanges of gifts between the two families, and feasting.

Death also brings the family together to mourn while the community offers support. The body of the deceased is washed and clothed by family members, then carried to the cremation ground in a procession. Hymns and prayers are offered. When the family returns home, there is usually a complete reading of the *Granth,* and mourners receive the familiar sweet, *karah parshad*. The sharing of food at this time symbolizes the continuity of social life, in contrast to the isolation that would be required of a Hindu family. Sikhs also consider this a time to contemplate the great good fortune involved in being born into the Sikh faith, where one may hear the words of the *gurus* and practice the *dharma* that leads to union with God. If a Sikh is a sincere believer, death is seen as the removal of the last obstacle separating him from God. One should remember that the real purpose of life is to make one's mind the abode of God, and thus the passing of a person who has lived according to the *dharma* is viewed as a time of joy, not sorrow.

Sikhism in California

The history of the Sikh religion in California may be divided into three phases. The first phase, from 1904–1923, was a period of immigration in which single men came to the United States seeking economic opportunities in order to help their families back in the Punjab. The second phase, from 1924 to 1946, delineates the era in which Asians were barred from immigration, and the small Sikh community remained fairly static. The third phase, from 1946 to the present, has seen a tremendous increase in the California Sikh population as immigration laws have changed once again. The settlement of these newest arrivals has been influenced by the experiences of their predecessors.

1904 to 1923: Early Migration

In the last years of the nineteenth century and the beginning of the twentieth, economic conditions in the Indian Punjab, the homeland of Sikhism, were deteriorating. The Punjab is a great alluvial plain in the northwestern corner of India, and at that time, three million peasants farmed small, irrigated land holdings and lived in villages of several hundred persons. At the end of the nineteenth century, there was a population explosion followed by droughts, famines, and severe epidemics. Although improved irrigation helped increase crop yields after 1900, and the growth of the railroads allowed farmers to sell surplus crops for profit, it was soon found that one of the best ways for the Sikh family to maintain prosperity was migration out of the area. Younger sons were sent off to find jobs away from the villages, thereby reducing the number of mouths to feed and increasing the families' outside sources of revenue. Some of these workers were veterans of the British army who chose not to reenlist after their first three-year tours of duty. By the beginning of the twentieth century, Punjabis could be found working far from the borders of India, in Asia and Africa. As opportunities in those areas grew fewer, Sikhs began to come to the Pacific coast of North America, attracted by higher wages and by the fact that men could immigrate as free workers instead of contract laborers.

Most of the workers who arrived in this first wave of Sikh migration were quite young, many in their early twenties. A few were married, but they left their wives and families behind in the Punjab. Most of the migrants came in clusters of relatives or were residents of the same village who would together plan a trip. Groups such as these, with communal and kinship ties along with common goals and a history of working together, had the best chance of succeeding in the new world. Often the army veterans within the migrant groups became the natural leaders because they wrote Punjabi and spoke some English.

The goal of these immigrants was simply to make money, and most of them hoped to work abroad temporarily before returning home to their families. The first Sikh migrants to North America worked in the Canadian timber mills for two dollars a day. Since this wage was far lower than that demanded by Euro-American workers, the mill owners were happy to replace their Euro-American laborers with Indians, whom they found to be good workers. Not surprisingly, tensions soon developed in the labor pool. After some Indian immigrants were attacked by whites, many of the workers began to move south into the United States. They found more timber work in Washington and Oregon, and even better wages laying out railroads in California.

By 1907, there were approximately two thousand Indians at work on the Western Pacific Railroad in California. At this time, the growing network of railroad lines was opening up large areas of northern California for national agricultural trade; farmers and ranchers could now ship goods by fast train to Chicago markets. This led to a boom in agricultural development, with farm workers receiving wages comparable to those previously paid by the railroads. Punjabis thus moved from railroad work into agricultural labor, where they were extraordinarily successful. Agriculture in the central California alluvial plain, with its irrigation projects and crop specialization, was similar to Punjabi agriculture, and Sikhs soon proved themselves to be valuable as knowledgeable field hands. Soon, Indians were settling in the San Joaquin, Sacramento, and Imperial valleys, where they adopted the profitable practice of land leasing and organized themselves into work gangs. Pooling their earnings and working together to lease land, many Sikhs had become successful tenant farmers by the 1920s. A 1919 census, for example, reported that Asian Indians occupied over 88,000 acres of land in California, half of it in the Sacramento Valley. Although Sikh surnames appear on records of deceased persons in twenty-nine counties from 1905 to 1929, suggesting that individual workers were spread throughout the state, fully three quarters of these were concentrated in the eleven counties of the San Joaquin, Sacramento, and Imperial valleys, where they could work in agriculture.

By 1914, Indians had begun to establish the community economic organizations that would bring them further success as landowners in America. Such organizations consisted of Sikh men living together and forming labor partnerships in which they worked as a unit and divided earnings equally. These collectives subsequently used their earnings to purchase small farms and orchards, which were tended in the evening by the members of the organization after their day labors were completed. Punjabi kinship and village ties formed the bases for these living groups and contributed to the trust necessary for their successful business relationships. By using the social ties of the old village community, Indians were thus able to survive and prosper in the competitive California agricultural market.

Some workers from this first wave of immigrants returned to India to raise families and live off the profits of their American ventures, while others chose to remain in the United States. The Indians were, however, isolated from the American mainstream by language and class barriers, as well as by a growing prejudice against all Asians that began to surface before World War I. Generally they kept to themselves, or joined Mexican-American or Black communities in California. A few Indian students did attend the University of California; they would often join their countrymen in the fields to work beside them and act as translators during the summer. The students told workers of the prejudice evoked by their turbans and recommended that they be put aside and that their long hair and beards be trimmed. Without turbans or long hair, the Sikhs could blend with Mexican workers and avoid confrontations.

In 1912, the Sikhs established the first *gurdwara* in the United States in Stockton, California. The original temple was a two-story wooden structure with an adjacent building that served as a dormitory for Sikh travelers. In 1929, the wooden structure was replaced with a brick building. The *gurdwara* served as a center for Sikh religion for the numerous laborers living in the San Joaquin area and also for workers who migrated through the area seasonally.

Attendance varied in accord with agricultural patterns and the difficulties of travel. Most Sikhs visited the temple four to six times a year, generally on major festival days such as Baisakhi (New Year's), Guru Arjan's martyrdom day, Guru Nanak's birthday, and Guru Gobind Singh's birthday. The *gurdwara* also served as the primary channel of communication with the Punjab and provided information on the independence movement in India, which was gaining momentum in the first decades of the twentieth century. Thus the *gurdwara* was not only a place of spiritual activities, but a cultural center where South Asians gathered in their shared identity as Indians. Punjabi Muslims were welcome to spread their prayer rugs in the *gurdwara* and share in the communal meals which are part of Sikh tradition.

As in the Punjab, the services in the *gurdwara* were organized around readings of the *Guru Granth Sahib*. Although the California migrants did not include any professionally trained readers, some of them could read the *gurmukhi* script in which the sacred text is written. Sikhs traveled from all over California to take part in the *gurdwara* festivals. The temple helped them preserve their community identity in a foreign land.

Unfortunately, the first wave of Indians who came to California had arrived on the heels of large migrations of Chinese and Japanese workers, who had inspired racist and economic fears among Euro-American laborers, leading to riots against the immigrants. The Sikhs themselves were perceived as the next Asian invasion and were labeled the "turbaned tide." Subsequent anti-Asian agitation led to the passage of laws in the 1920s that stopped Asian immigration and barred Asians from owning land in California. A separate court ruling in 1923—the infamous Thind case—declared Indians ineligible for citizenship, even though they were considered Caucasian, not Asian.

The discrimination from outside their community undoubtedly added to the Sikhs' sense of unity and solidified their connection with their Indian roots. These were further strengthened by the growth of a California-based Indian political movement called the Ghadar party, which sought Indian independence from British rule. *Ghadar* means "revolution" in Punjabi, and both Hindu and Sikh Punjabis were active in the movement. The first leader of the party in California was a Punjabi Hindu named Lala Har Dayal, who relied heavily on the rural Sikh population for financial support of his activities. The immigrant experience of Sikhs overseas seems to have exacerbated their desire for freedom from British rule back home. The struggle to live in a foreign culture had added to a sense of Indian identity and a desire for autonomy from foreign rule, but, perhaps more than this, overseas Indians were convinced that the reason they were so poorly regarded by other countries was that they were a subject nation. In fact, in the Thind case of 1923, the courts did deny naturalized citizenship to South Asians based on the premise that they were not "free white persons." The Indians thus believed that they would be treated better both abroad and at home if they were citizens of a free and sovereign nation of India.

The subsequent breakdown of the Ghadar party after World War I shows a growing disunity among the Indian immigrants. While the Punjabi Har Dayal was leader, the Sikhs were active supporters of the movement. When the leadership shifted to a non-Punjabi Hindu, the divisions between the urban Hindu intellectuals and the rural Sikh agriculturalists became more pronounced. The attempts to lead revolutionary activities in India had not been successful, and many Sikhs, both in India and overseas, were beginning to feel that independence was not going to be so easy to achieve. The most radical Punjabis had already returned to India to fight for independence, leaving the more settled workers in California. Many of those who remained in the United States had been here long enough to have a real interest in their immediate environment and little desire to return to India.

1924 to 1946

During the period after 1923, when Indians were declared ineligible for citizenship, the California Sikh community was in general decline. The changes in immigration laws had made it nearly impossible for Indians to enter the United States and, although there was a trickle of illegal immigration through Mexico, even that slowed once the country entered the Depression after 1928. By the mid-1930s, the Indian community was a static group. People might return to India, especially as the independence movement grew, but no new immigrants came to America.

Many of the original immigrants had already returned to India. Those who remained were trapped by circumstances. Not only did the new laws make it impossible for them to visit their families in India, since it would not be possible to return to the United States, but because their families continued to need the extra income they provided, they had to remain. Indeed, some had become very successful in their agricultural endeavors. Even though they could not legally own land, they managed to work around the laws by employing other people as proxy owners.

As the prospect of return to India faded and the men passed from youth to middle age, many of them formed families. About half of the Sikh immigrants married while in California. There were very few Indian women in the United States and most were already married, so the Sikhs had to look elsewhere for brides. The few Indians living in urban areas usually married Euro-American women, while the majority of the rural Sikhs married Mexican women, especially in southern California. Apparently the agricultural success of the Sikhs made them popular marriage material.

The new families did not, however, continue Punjabi Sikh traditions. The children spoke English and often some Spanish, but rarely learned Punjabi, even though many of their fathers tried to teach them. Most of the children were baptized as Christians by their mothers and grew up attending church services. In India, the grandparents do most of the religious education and socializing of the children, but this generation was not present in California to make Sikh traditions part of daily life. Furthermore, in the traditional Sikh household, the daily prayers and practices are most often performed by the mother, but in these California families the mothers were Christians. The Sikh fathers did attend religious meetings and read the *Guru Granth Sahib*, but all the reading and discussion was in Punjabi, so even when the children were taken to services, they could not participate. Moreover, the men refused to adapt their religion to English because they needed to preserve their traditions as they remembered them in the Punjab in order to affirm their cultural identity. Given this situation, Sikhism would probably have disappeared from California as soon as the older generation died, had not the immigration laws changed in 1946.

1946 to present

In 1946, the Luce-Cellar bill passed in the U.S. Congress, thereby giving persons of East Indian descent the right to become United States citizens. The new law also set a quota of one hundred immigrants per year from India, which, while low, nevertheless made it possible to bring family members over from South Asia for the first time. At this point, there were fewer than 1,500 South Asians in the entire country, but the number began to slowly increase as those who had been successful in the United States sent home for wives and brides.

Meanwhile, back in South Asia, India achieved independence

from Great Britain in 1947, although in the process it was divided
into two countries, India and Pakistan. The dividing line between
the two countries ran right through the Punjab and, suddenly, the
Punjabi Sikhs and Muslims were forced to relocate across the newly
created border. The partition of India had two major consequences
in California. First, many of the East Indians in California found
themselves permanently displaced as their ancestral homes were
now gone. The partition had a similar effect on the Punjabi Muslims
in California. Second, the partition changed the relationship
between these two immigrant groups. During the years of labor in a
foreign land, the common language and culture of the Punjabi Sikhs
and Muslims had given them a sense of community and contributed
to the formation of close friendships. These survived after the partition, but became more difficult to sustain as immigrants who had
been involved in the partition conflict back in India began to arrive
in California. Punjabi Muslims slowly stopped dropping by the
Stockton *gurdwara*, a trend that was hastened by the formation of
Muslim centers that provided them with their own houses of worship.

The partition also added to the Sikh sense of identity as a group
separate from the Hindu Indians. This identity, although supported
by the regional linguistic ties of the Punjab, was centered around the
Sikh religion. As South Asian groups established their own religious
centers in California, the old camaraderie of the early migrants, who
had met in largely ecumenical cultural gatherings, faded. For example, in 1948 the Sikhs of the Imperial Valley decided they needed a
place of worship closer to home than Stockton, so they bought a
Japanese Buddhist temple and converted it to a *gurdwara*. This gave
the Sikhs a local center of Sikh worship, but also meant that they no
longer took part in events with South Asian Muslims and Hindus in
the area. In response, the Muslims formed their own Pakistan Club.

The resumption of immigration after 1946 was very slow; fewer
than 200 people came each year before 1959. But the new laws at
least allowed for the reconstitution of families, and this considerably
changed the structure of the communities. Men could now go to
India to get married, or they could bring wives and children, whom
they had not seen for years, over to California. Most of the new Sikh
immigrants came to the more northern parts of the state. The southern Sikh community in the Imperial Valley, which had never been
large, did not benefit from increased immigration because shifts in
the economics of desert farming no longer made it profitable for
Sikhs to settle there.

Although the number of immigrants in the 1950s was not large, they had a tremendous impact on the California Sikh culture. These new immigrants wore the clothing and spoke the language of the Punjab and were firmly committed to traditional Sikhism. Most of the men maintained the five Ks. The influx of more overtly Sikh practices caused a few of the old-timers to re-adopt traditional behavior, and this led to an extended dialogue in the California Sikh community over issues of orthodoxy, ritualism vs. liberalism, and questions about what it meant to be a Sikh. These issues and questions would become even more important as the newcomers began to outnumber their predecessors in the 1970s.

In 1965, President Johnson further relaxed the immigration laws. By this time the economic standing of the East Indian families already in California was so well improved that they were able to sponsor the immigration of more relatives. Some of the Sikhs in the Sacramento area had become remarkably successful, especially as growers of cling peaches. Sikhs who owned farm land could sponsor immigrants and put them to work in the peach industry. The Sikh community north of Stockton, where most of these farmers lived, grew so large that they built their own *gurdwara* in 1969 in Yuba City. The new temple is much larger than the old Stockton center. But the Stockton *gurdwara* still has a special symbolic appeal to American Sikhs and is very crowded during the Baisakhi festival, when Sikhs come from all over California, Nevada, and even Arizona and Oregon to celebrate at the first temple in the United States.

Prior to the 1960s, Sikhism in California had been fairly relaxed. Readings of the *Guru Granth Sahib* had been held occasionally at private homes and at the Stockton *gurdwara*, but not often. The life-cycle rites, such as the child's naming, birth celebrations, initiation into the Khalsa, and weddings, were extremely rare. Only funerals and memorial services were frequent, religiously reflecting the actualities of life at the time. Some of the Sikh immigrants knew their scriptures and could read the *gurmukhi* script, but none of them were trained *granthi*s. Traditionally, the criteria for selecting a *granthi* included a willingness to serve, ability to read *gurmukhi* script, good moral character, and evidence of having kept the five Ks for life. In California after 1935, this last requirement was changed so that the five Ks need only be maintained for the duration of one's service as *granthi*.

The building of the Yuba City *gurdwara* brought about a great change in the religious habits of the Sikh community located there.

All the major religious festivals and services are now observed, including those which celebrate birthdays, martyrdoms, and significant events in the lives of the Sikh *gurus*. The temple also now has daily morning and evening services. Indeed, the entire range of life-cycle rites has been reinstituted. This is not a peculiarity of the Sacramento region. New *gurdwara*s have also been built in the San Francisco Bay Area and in Los Angeles. The Sikh community in California is no longer just a handful of farmers in a few scattered areas, but now constitutes a large enough cultural group to maintain the practices that are central to the religion in the Punjab.

As the number of recent immigrants has grown, the balance of opinion in the *gurdwara*s has shifted from the relaxed attitudes of the earlier immigrants to the more orthodox ideals of the newcomers. This has brought some changes in the outward practices of the religion in California. In the late 1940s, for example, Americanized Sikhs had placed chairs in the Stockton *gurdwara* and allowed people to keep their shoes on and their heads uncovered in the temple. These practices have since been discontinued, and the behavior in the *gurdwara* has reverted to the Indianized forms, shoeless, with covered heads and people seated on the floor in gender-segregated areas.

This return to orthodoxy was not, however, made without some protest from the old-timers. At times they accused the new immigrants of practicing "Singhism," focusing too much on the teaching of Guru Gobind Singh and not enough on the original precepts set forth by Guru Nanak. They argued that the rules for the Khalsa laid out by Gobind Singh were meant to meet the needs of a specific time and place, and were no longer appropriate. They preferred to emphasize the religious teachings of Nanak, which stressed devotion and peace, and de-emphasize external ritual elements like dress codes and observance of the five Ks. The division between these factions was strong enough that, in 1980, the old-timers opened their own *gurdwara* in Yuba City, calling it the Guru Nanak Sikh Temple. Here morning and evening services are held every day, and weekend services are held on Sunday mornings. Despite the original intentions behind the construction of this second *gurdwara*, the orthodox community grew to outnumber the older population and, by the late 1980s, the practices at this second temple had been brought in line with those at the other *gurdwara*.

Today, the Sikh agricultural community in the northern part of the state has grown so large that it forms its own sub-community within the region. These Sikhs have very little need to interact with their non-Punjabi neighbors, except for a few retail transactions. They own their own businesses, employ other Punjabis, socialize among themselves, and discourage their children from spending time with people from outside the community. The cohesion of the Sikh community here is enhanced by kinship ties. The reason so many have migrated to the northern valleys is that they were sponsored by family members already engaged in farming there. Thus, whole extended families from India, including married siblings with their offspring, have been reconstituted in the valleys of northern California. The very size of this homogeneous group facilitates their ability to maintain their own cultural identity. Sikhs have begun to branch out from the agricultural occupations that served the first immigrants so well, but most of these new occupations have connections with agriculture. For example, Sikhs now sell fertilizer and farm equipment, which is purchased by other Sikhs who are still working the land. Sikh shopkeepers supply commercial goods like traditional clothing and spices that are imported from India. As the number of Sikhs residing in northern California has grown, they have had less and less need to go outside the community for day-to-day needs. The occasional experiences of racism from Anglo-Americans have contributed to the insulation of the Punjabi community, but most Sikhs speak positively about the Anglos they know personally and do not feel that all Americans are racist. They ascribe such incidents to a natural resentment of newcomers who seem to be succeeding with ease.

In the 1970s and 1980s, Sikhs settled throughout the state. Although the largest communities are still made up of agriculturalists or people working in businesses associated with the agricultural community, there is also a growing urban Sikh population in California. These city-dwellers have not formed an isolated community with a transplanted culture like that of the rural Punjabis in the northern counties. The Sikhs who have settled in urban areas are mostly highly educated professionals, many of whom came as students, or members of the American-educated second generation who chose non-agricultural career paths. They work as dentists, teachers, doctors, and engineers. They neither live nor work in close proximity to each other and do not have the extended kinship networks that provide such cohesion for the agricultural population. Their urban environment and the smaller size of the Sikh population in California cities make it necessary for them to interact with non-Indians more often. The second generation, in particular, is much more a part of the mainstream culture than their agriculturalist parents. And yet, these urban Sikhs have also pooled their resources to build centralized *gurdwara*s which link them together as a community. Even though they do not live in the same neighborhoods, work in the same offices, or try to insulate their traditional lifestyles from the mainstream, they still have a strong sense of identity as members of the Sikh Khalsa. The *gurdwara* serves as a focal center, especially during the weekend services and the special celebrations, when large crowds gather.

In 1990, there were eighteen *gurdwara*s in California. These temples are multi-purpose facilities. The primary focus is, of course, the large meeting hall that houses the *Guru Granth Sahib*, but each *gurdwara* also has a library with a collection of Punjabi materials that is available to everyone. Larger temples have additional rooms in which they offer classes in Punjabi language and dance. There are also large kitchens and storage facilities for preparing the communal meals that are such an integral part of Sikhism. The continuous interjection of new immigrants into the community keeps the Sikhs tied to the traditional practices of the Punjab. Because the Sikh religion is centered around a particular body of teachings, it has proven itself to be highly portable and has been transplanted to the United States fairly well. It is, nevertheless, closely bound to a larger Punjabi identity and culture that can only partially be recreated in another country. Thus, it is sometimes difficult for Sikh children to reconcile some of the more traditional social ideals of the Punjab, such as the obedience required of wives and the idea of arranged marriages, with the mainstream American cultural values to which they are exposed in school. And, in spite of the greater size of the contemporary community, modern California Sikh children still have the same problem with language as the second generation of Sikh offspring had in the 1930s and 1940s—they are rarely fluent in Punjabi. Most of the children do speak the language, but they cannot read the *gurmukhi* script. This severely curtails their ability to participate in study of the *Guru Granth Sahib*, which is at the heart of the Sikh tradition. Professional readers can make up for this deficiency in *gurdwara* services and during special events, but the inability to read from the *Granth* is a problem for household religious practices. Moreover, most people do not feel a great need to focus on religious practices in the home until they have children of their own. Thus, despite the fact that classes in Punjabi are offered at the *gurdwara*, the second generation will probably remain ignorant of the language until they begin to form families, if ever.

An additional problem for traditional Sikhism in California is that most American-raised children cease to keep the five Ks before they reach high school because peer pressure is too powerful. This is true both in the rural communities, with their large Punjabi populations, and in the urban areas. Thus, the second generation are not *keshdari*, that is, they do not keep the five Ks. Nevertheless, the term "Sikh" still applies to them because the term has come to denote an individual from a Sikh family who is part of the larger Punjabi cultural tradition, even if he or she does not practice the religion. Such "cultural" Sikhs, who have been part of the tradition since the days of the tenth *guru*, are not considered members of the Khalsa because they have not gone through the initiation ritual, but they still identify themselves with the Punjabi community. Many Sikh children in California fall into this category because they are very proud of their Punjabi heritage and have no desire to throw it aside for total assimilation into American culture. They may reject the stricter rules of behavior about male-female interactions and arranged marriages, but they place great value on the ideals their parents have taught them. Their sense of identity with their Punjabi heritage is further enhanced by the modern era of telecommunications and air travel. The American-reared children of immigrants are able to gain firsthand knowledge of their parents' homeland by making regular visits to grandparents in India. Thus, modern technology is helping to maintain the ties between California Sikhs and the Punjab.

The strength of these ties has been quite apparent of late in the reaction among California Sikhs to the recent troubles in the Punjab. The conflict between the Sikhs and the Indian government has been hard on American Sikhs. When news that the Indian government had invaded the Golden Temple at Amritsar to capture some Sikh rebels reached Sikhs in America, it sparked protest marches and calls for the U.S. government to condemn such wanton desecration of a religious shrine. Moreover, the horror of the riots in India which followed the assassination of Indira Gandhi by her Sikh bodyguards left many Sikhs desperate to find out what had happened to family members. The renewed conflict with the Indian government has served to strengthen the sense of "Punjabi" identity for the California Sikh population. They remain deeply concerned with events in the homeland of their tradition.

Bibliography

Cameron, C. "Pilgrims and Politics: Sikh Gurdwaras in California." In *Pilgrimage in the United States*. Berlin: Dietrich Reimer Verlag, 1990.

Chakravorti, Robindra C. *The Sikhs of El Centro: A Study in Social Integration*. Thesis. University of Minnesota, 1968.

Chandrasekhar, S., editor. *From India to America*. La Jolla: Population Review, 1982.

Cole, W. Owen, and Sambhi, Piara Singh. *The Sikhs: Their Religious Beliefs and Practices*. London: Routledge & Kegan Paul, 1978.

Dhillon, Mahinder Singh. *The Sikhs in Canada and California*. Vancouver: Shromani Akali Dal Association of Canada, 1981.

Fleuret, Anne K. "Incorporation into Networks Among Sikhs in Los Angeles." In *Urban Anthropology*. Vol. 3 (1), 1974: 27–33.

Gibson, M.A. *Accommodation without Assimilation: Sikh Immigrants in an American High School*. New York: Cornell University Press, 1988.

Jensen, Joan M. *Passage from India: Asian Indian Immigrants in North America*. New Haven: Yale University Press, 1988.

Jha, Ajit Kumar. "A Community of Discord." In *India Today*. Nov. 15, 1992: 48b–48e.

La Brack, Bruce. *The Sikhs of Northern California*: 1904–1975. New York: AMS Press, 1988.

McLeod, W.H. *The Sikhs: History, Religion, and Society*. New York: Columbia University Press, 1989.

Misrow, Jogesh C. *East Indian Immigration on the Pacific Coast*. Stanford, 1915.

Sikh Religion. Detroit: Sikh Missionary Center, 1990.

Singh, Ganda. *The Sikhs and Their Religion*. Redwood City: The Sikh Foundation, 1974.

Singh, Gopal. *The Religion of the Sikhs*. London: Asia Publishing House, 1971.

State Board of Control. *California and the Oriental: Japanese, Chinese, and Hindus*. Sacramento: California State Printing Office, 1922.

Thursby, Gene R. *The Sikhs*. Iconography of Religions Series. New York: E.J. Brill, 1992.

Williams, Raymond Brady. *Religions of Immigrants from India and Pakistan*. Cambridge: Cambridge University Press, 1988.

3 Hinduism: Unity and Diversity

One day in 1989, some Hindus discovered that a Shiva *lingam* had appeared in Golden Gate Park, San Francisco. The *lingam*, a domed pillar, is the aniconic image that represents the presence of the god Shiva. The stone had appeared at a crossroads among the trails through the park, near the stones of a disassembled monastery. The Hindus, who walked through the park frequently, knew that the *lingam* had not been there the previous day and they hastened to tell others about the miraculous event. Soon, people began to visit the park to worship the emblem of Shiva. A Hindu deity had manifested itself in California.

Hinduism

Unlike most of the western religions, Hinduism has no one teacher or text, and no clear historical starting point. It emerged over centuries out of the interaction of priestly ritual traditions, devotional movements, and popular sects. The people who identify themselves as Hindus speak sixteen major languages (and countless dialects), pray to "three hundred and thirty million" different deities, and belong to diverse regional-linguistic cultures—each with its own variations on ritual, festival, and doctrine. There are certain key beliefs that tie the many "Hinduisms" together, but the practical manifestation of those beliefs varies across India and around the world.

The Introduction described some core beliefs that are shared by most Hindus. Life is perceived as cyclical and the individual's rebirths are determined by the actions of the preceding lifetime. Hindus believe that there are many names for the divine but only one underlying Absolute, and, in the same way, there are many religious paths but only one ultimate goal. These various paths exist to meet the needs of people from different social classes who have diverse psychological tendencies, so that all may have a chance to reach the highest knowledge by the means most appropriate to the individual. *Dharma*, the word for religion, which also means order, law, and duty, includes all these different paths. This is a central tenet of Hinduism—to be religious is to live according to proper codes of behavior and to perform the duties of life appropriate to one's place within the larger context of society. In this way, religion is tied to traditional lifestyles and social duties, but the actual practices are personal. Even though there are great public festivals in India, Hinduism is not really a congregational tradition. The act of being religious is internal, it is a way of life and a personal quest for knowledge of the presence of the divine in everyday life. The way one is to live out one's religious precepts is elucidated by the local tradition to which one belongs. This tradition is usually centered around a particular temple or deity and a particular teaching tradition passed down through a lineage of monks and *gurus* (teachers) who interpret the scriptures and tell people how to apply them to daily life.

The professional religious may be divided into two categories: priests and renunciates. The priests are those who perform the rituals at the temples. They are members of families that have held these positions for generations and who must receive careful education in the proper performance of rituals and hymns. Renunciates are those who have given up all social position and family life to search for divine truth. They may live as ascetic hermits, devoting their lives to physical and mental practices that will help them attain knowledge of the true nature of the divine and break out of the cycle of rebirth. Or they may take monastic vows and join specific religious orders. Some monks spend their lives in service and meditation, others wander around India traveling from shrine to shrine. Many of these are teachers who will give instruction to people in the towns they visit. Such a monk may permanently settle near a town and become the village holy man. Traditionally it has been the monks who provided religious instruction to village folk, not the temple priests. The priests are generally perceived as people performing a job for which they have been trained and for which they receive monetary rewards, not as true holy men. The man (or woman) of real faith is one who has given up all attachments to worldly goods, and who devotes his or her whole life to pursuing the connection with God. These people need not be professional religious. Indeed, the great saints of India have come from every walk of life—they have been ascetics, weavers, untouchables, housewives, and priests—but all have spent their lives totally absorbed in God.

Hindus describe the pattern of life as divided into four natural stages. The first quarter of one's life is spent as a student. The student should focus on learning a trade and mastering the basic precepts of religion. Next, one becomes a householder. The householder should marry and work to support a family, to raise children and provide for their security, to support his or her parents, and to establish a respected place in the community. Then, when one reaches middle age, and the children are married and have become self-sufficient, it is time to turn over the family business to the next generation and withdraw from the distractions of worldly life. This is the stage of the "forest-dweller," named after the old practice of retiring from village life to live in a forest hermitage. Nowadays, however, people usually continue to live with their children in the family home, practicing a spiritual retirement rather than removing themselves bodily from society. They spend more time going to the local temple, perhaps making pilgrimages to holy sites, and they generally turn their minds toward contemplation of religious matters. This retired generation introduces their grandchildren to religion by taking them to the temple and recounting tales of the gods and epic heroes.

Finally, there is a fourth stage of complete renunciation for those who wish to separate themselves from all worldly connections and devote themselves fully to meditation and religious discipline. Ideally, this fourth stage is only for those who have completed all their obligations to continue their family line by going through the householder stage. In reality though, those who feel the call to devote their lives to seeking the Absolute may come from any age group. These are the people who join monastic orders and become wandering monks and hermits.

Both professional religious folk and laity may choose from among the different religious paths which have been enumerated over the years in India and have come to be accepted as alternative methods of religious observance appropriate for different lifestyles and psychological types. People who have leisure time and an intellectual bent may follow the path of knowledge called Jnana-yoga, which emphasizes study of scripture and meditation. For those who prefer an emotional connection to God, the path of devotion, Bhakti-yoga, emphasizes loving worship which brings one into communion with God. Karma-yoga, the path of action, advocates doing all work as an offering to God without attachment to the fruits of one's labors. It is believed that actions performed without attachment do not produce *karma*. Raja-yoga, the royal path, stresses the importance of meditation to penetrate the veils of ignorance and to realize the true nature of the self. It is important to recognize that no one of these paths is exclusive: A person may approach God with feelings of great love, perform his daily work as an offering, read scriptures, and practice meditation. Most Hindus in India belong to a local teaching tradition that draws on a combination of these different paths.

Gods and Goddesses

Although most Hindus worship many gods and goddesses, they will also tell you that there is really only one God (which is neither masculine nor feminine). The multitude of deities is described as diverse forms of the great gods, and the great gods are also perceived as various manifestations of the one God. An individual usually has one particular god or goddess, called his or her chosen deity, to whom he or she directs prayers. But this does not mean that he or she will neglect the annual festivals in honor of other deities. One may offer a prayer to the god Shiva in the morning; request the blessings of Lakshmi, the goddess of fortune, at the office; ask for the aid of Sarasvati, patroness of learning, during an exam; and celebrate the birth of Krishna at midnight on his anniversary festival.

Almost every temple in India has its own special image, and there are as many different images of God as there are places to worship. Most of these images are considered forms of three major deities: Vishnu, Shiva, and Devi. Of these, Vishnu is the most popular deity in India. His mythology centers around his incarnations, the most celebrated of which are Krishna and Rama. According to tradition, Vishnu is the god who works to preserve order in the cosmos. Whenever there is an imbalance of powers, he takes on a material form and enters his creation in order to set things right. Vishnu was incarnated on earth as Rama to free people from the cruel dominion of a demon and to establish righteous (dharmic) order in the world. He then took on the form of Krishna, the cowherd, to ensure the correct outcome of a great battle of the rulers in India and, perhaps more importantly, to bring a new teaching about devotion to God as the highest form of religion. This new emphasis on devotion brought by Vishnu in his guise as Krishna is supposed to be the religious path best suited for people living in the dark age, our present time, which is the last stage in the current cycle of the cosmos.

For most worshippers of Vishnu, the emphasis on devotion presupposes a belief in a personal god who is separate from his devotees. Through meritorious living and devotion, Vaishnavas (devotees of Vishnu) hope to spend eternity in Vishnu's presence. In his temples, Vishnu is usually depicted in the forms of his famous incarnations, like Rama and Krishna, or as a magnificent king wearing a crown and carrying emblems of power. Most of his devotees have images of him in at least one of his incarnations in their homes.

Shaivites (devotees of Shiva), on the other hand, usually conceive of God as an impersonal force that is the underlying substance and cause of the cosmos. Shiva is a god of paradoxes. He is the great yogic ascetic, who spends a thousand years in meditation detached from the world, yet he is also represented in his temples by the phallic *lingam*, symbol of his role as creator of the cosmos. Whereas Vishnu is the celestial king who upholds order, Shiva is the ascetic who transcends social laws. This is not, however, a contradiction in the Hindu belief system. Asceticism generates great power, including erotic power, and power may be both creative and destructive. Shaivism emphasizes the awesome power and otherness of God by describing Shiva as both creator and destroyer. The popular image of the dancing Shiva encircled by fire represents the dance of destruction. But this destruction is also the prelude to the recreation of the cosmos. Similarly, Shiva's destructive force may be used to benefit devotees as the Lord destroys negative *karma* and human weaknesses for the sake of his followers. Shaivites approach their god with the same devotion as Vaishnavas, but their religious practices also tend to incorporate traditions of meditation and yogic discipline associated with their *yogin* deity.

Devi, the Great Goddess, is also an embodiment of the polarities of divine power. She is both the mother who gives birth to all life and the fierce protectress who can lay waste entire armies when roused to wrath. Usually her destructive power is aimed at forces that threaten the world or at the negative tendencies of her devotees. The fiercest image of the Goddess shows her as Kali, a figure with black skin, fangs, and lolling tongue, who wears a garland of skulls and a skirt of severed arms. Despite the seemingly horrific aspect of this goddess, Kali's devotees understand her ferocity as a positive representation of her power. They say that the skulls symbolize negative human tendencies, like greed and selfishness, and that the arms represent the *karma* of her devotees, which she removes from them out of compassion. Those who worship the Great Goddess call her Mother and approach her with loving devotion, whether she is depicted as the fair Parvati holding one of her children on her lap, or as the regal warrior goddess, Durga, riding her lion and carrying myriad weapons.

All goddesses are considered forms of the one Great Goddess, and there are shrines to local female deities in almost every village in India. The Goddess is associated with the earth and fertility; the life-giving waters of the rivers are also personified as goddesses. Indeed, the entire Indian sub-continent is often described as an embodiment of Devi. One myth tells how the body of the goddess was cut into pieces and scattered across the land; the shrines in India mark the places where the fragments of her body fell. Reverence for the Goddess pervades India. Lakshmi, the goddess of prosperity and good fortune, is depicted on Indian money. Sarasvati, the goddess of learning, is honored at a special festival in schools every year. And one of the biggest celebrations of the year, the Navaratri, is a nine-day harvest festival in honor of the Goddess in various forms during the fall.

These great deities, who preside over the entire cosmos, are generally thought to distance themselves from mundane problems. Hindus rarely ask them for help with the difficulties that arise in ordinary life such as drought, epidemic, illness, or childlessness. In fact, it is generally felt that the great deities would be angered if people tried to persuade them to act in specific ways. For these matters, Hindus turn to other deities who have more specialized functions or more local characters.

There are numerous village deities who are associated with particular places, families, or forces. Most towns have a village goddess, who is the protector of the community, and there are gods and goddesses who serve as patrons of various crafts or help with specfic problems like conception and childbirth. Many of these "little deities" have non-divine origins. They may have been malevolent ghosts of people who died prematurely and lingered in the world to harass the living, but through worship their spirits were placated and their powers, which were once harmful, became beneficial. Heroes who died in battle and heroines who immolated themselves on their husbands' funeral pyres might also become local deities.

The village gods and goddesses, divinized spirits, and ghosts do not have large temples presided over by upper-class priests. They are worshipped at simple sites, sometimes merely a red-painted rock, a tree, a spring, or even a pot of water. Often the tomb of a local hero or a saint becomes a shrine. Human beings who become deities are considered to be particularly understanding of the needs of ordinary people, especially members of their own families or former community. But the power of these small gods and goddesses is usually limited. Most of them are only called on to help with local matters like procuring sons or fending off agricultural problems. They do not play a role in ultimate issues such as ensuring that people attain a better rebirth after death.

Worship

Puja is the core ritual of worship in Hinduism. It is performed before deities' images in temples and homes by priests and by lay folk. The central elements of *puja* involve welcoming the deity and honoring the god or goddess as an adored guest. The deity is offered water to drink, its image is undressed and bathed, and then given fresh clothing and decked in flowers. Food is offered and entertainment provided in the form of music, singing, and dancing. Incense purifies the air and oil lamps are waved before the deity. At the end of the *puja*, the deity is bid farewell and the devotees bow in a gesture of respect. By means of the ritual, devotees honor and express personal affection for the gods and goddesses.

Puja is performed in temples on a daily basis and, in simplified form, in homes daily or weekly. Most homes have a household shrine where images or pictures of deities are kept. Men participate, especially during important festivals, but women are responsible for most of the domestic worship, particularly in south India. *Puja* is also the core event in major festivals, but these also include processions, singing, making offerings to a ritual fire, and sometimes animal sacrifice.

Individually, people may practice yogic exercises of physical discipline and meditation, through prescribed postures and breath control. These exercises are an aid to gaining control of the mind so that one may contemplate the true nature of existence and become aware of God. Study of religious texts, chanting, singing songs of praise, and repetition of a *mantra* (a syllable or phrase that embodies the Divine) are also part of regular religious practice. Ideally, each person should begin the day before dawn by remembering God and by mentally offering all of the work to be done that day to God. Offering up one's labors turns everyday work into an act of worship. Prayers should be offered in the family *puja* room before breakfast, and *mantras* may be recited throughout the day. *Puja* should then be performed again in the evening before dinner.

The *samskaras*, often called the sacraments of Hinduism, are rites that guide the Hindu along the path of *dharma*, of virtuous living. These ceremonies combine the elements of *puja*, prayer, utterance of ancient hymns, and communal feasting. Birth, initiation, marriage, and death, are the most frequently observed rites. The ceremonies that surround the birth of a child include sponsoring *pujas* at the temple and reciting prayers of petition for a long life attended by good fortune. Special celebrations may be held to mark a child's birth, naming, eating of first solid food, and first haircut. The initiation ritual marks a child's entry into the student stage of life. It was originally held for boys of the three higher castes, but today is common only with the *brahmins* (priests). The boy is dressed in ritual garments and brought to a teacher of the ancient Vedic lore, who invests him with the sacred thread (a triple strand of three threads to be worn over the right shoulder) and gives him his first lesson. Most families keep in contact with a traditional teacher who instructs the boys in the *dharma* appropriate to their family life. Marriage rites differ from region to region, but most include prayers, circumambulation of a fire altar, and utterance of auspicious *mantras* by a priest. The wedding prayers ask for strength in adversity, health, children, long life, and faith in each other. These are the ingredients of a good life. The ceremony culminates in a great feast.

At death, the family prepares the body of the deceased, carries it in procession to the cremation grounds, and recites specific hymns while the body is cremated. The god of death is called upon to give the deceased a good place among the ancestors, and other deities are also invoked to intercede on behalf of the departed loved one. Once cremated, the ashes and bones of the deceased are either committed to a river or buried. Renunciates and small children are usually buried without cremation. After the funeral the family members go to a brook or river to purify themselves with ritual baths. Because of the death, the family will be in a state of ritual impurity for a prescribed amount of time and will have to limit interactions with others. Every month for the first year after the death of one's parents, the son must perform the Shraddha rite for his ancestors. This rite centers around offerings of nourishment and prayers for the welfare of the deceased relatives. After a year passes, the rite is performed annually. Because this rite is the duty of the son, Indians set great importance on the birth of a male child.

These formal temple rituals are complemented by numerous regional folk practices, which are oriented around the well-being of the family and community. Most of these involve the performance of rites to gain the attention of local deities, either to gain benefits from them or to placate them and keep them from causing harm. Women, for example, will make offerings to local goddesses in order to get pregnant. Women also have the ability to ensure the health and well-being of their families by fasting on certain days. If someone does become ill or there is some trouble in the household, family members may promise to make a pilgrimage or pay for the construction of a shrine in order to gain the aid of a deity. Malevolent spirits such as unhappy ghosts may be identified as the source of problems such as drought or crop damage in a village, and the community will perform rituals and make offerings to placate them. There are also deities associated with diseases who must be propitiated to avoid illness or to bring an end to an epidemic. These regional practices directed at local deities are variations on the pan-Indian temple rituals—they involve prayers and praise of deities accompanied by offerings and promises to live in accord with the laws of social morality.

Darshana

It is important to understand the place of the temple and household images in Hinduism. When Hindus visit a temple, they are there for *darshana* "vision," that is, they come to see the deities and to be seen by them. The image in the temple is an embodiment of the actual deity. Through the ritual of consecration, the deity's power is installed in the image, so that the stone or wood is pervaded with his or her manifest presence. There is, of course, no limit to the number of images within which the deity's power can be installed, since the image is not the totality of the deity. It is better to say that the deity is *in* the image and devotees who gaze on the image are touched by the power flowing through it. So, for the Hindu, the divine is actually present in the image, but is not limited to that image.

Temples have sculpted images of their tutelary deities. The main image is usually made out of stone or caste in bronze according to traditional rules about the proper form for a particular god or goddess. Temples also have smaller images which can be carried in annual festivals. Some festivals require special images made of clay that are dissolved in rivers or the ocean at the end of the celebration. After they are consecrated, these man-made images are considered sacred, since the presence of God is now resident in them; but that presence is only temporary, and when the image dissolves the divine presence merges back into the infinite. Hindus speak reverently of the miraculous grace God bestows on them when he takes on embodied forms. Without these forms, his devotees would be incapable of comprehending his all-pervasive, unmanifest Nature.

There are also natural images, in which God's presence is self-existent, without a priestly consecration ritual. Among these are aniconic rocks that have been recognized as Shiva *lingam*s, and the fossil known as the *shalagrama* that is sacred to Vishnu. Aniconic images such as unhewn rocks painted red or pots of sanctified water often serve as images for the little deities in villages throughout India. Recently, color prints have become the most popular images for household use, and these are now consecrated and worshipped in homes just like the sculpted images.

There are also Hindus who decry the use of images and maintain that God is ultimately formless and without qualities. Devotees of God without attributes focus on recitation of the name of God and contemplation of the otherness of the Divine. Some see the worship of images as a preliminary stage to aid those who are not yet able to comprehend the impersonal nature of God. These Hindus believe that the reverence for the image should eventually be given up as one realizes that the divine presence is all-pervasive. For them, believing that God is more present in one place than another is to mistakenly attribute limitations to the Absolute.

Prasada

After acts of worship, devotees receive *prasada*, which literally means "grace." There are several different ways of receiving *prasada*. For example, the priest may bring the camphor flame that has been waved before the image to the devotees, who cup their hands over the flame and then touch their fingertips to their eyes. Through this act, the benevolent protective grace of the deity is transmitted to the worshiper and absorbed through the eyes. In Shiva temples, white ash and red powder are handed out, which the devout normally put on their foreheads. In Vishnu temples, people receive a little consecrated water, some of which they sprinkle on their heads and some of which they swallow. People may also receive water that has been used to bathe the image, or flowers that were placed on the image during the ritual. Often the main type of *prasada* is food that has been offered to the deity during worship.

Prasada is the material symbol of the deity's power and grace.

During *puja*, these substances have been transferred to the deity, either through contact with the image or, in the case of food, by being symbolically consumed by the deity. *Prasada* substances have thus been imbued with divine power and grace, which can then be absorbed by the devotee who receives them.

Sacred Sites

Every temple and shrine in India has its own presiding deity, but these are described as different forms of the great gods, or simply as different names for the great gods. Almost every temple has its own legend about how the deity once came to that location. The legends draw on mythical themes and explain how Vishnu, Shiva, or Devi, in a particular form, chose to situate himself or herself at that temple site. Thus, the site is made sacred through the presence of the deity.

Pilgrimage in India means a visit to a "crossing place," a place where there is a link between the divine and human worlds. Many of these "crossing places" are the sites of large temples, which, according to Indian mythology, mark locations where deities have appeared on earth. Each site has a legend to explain how the deity came there and what benefits, transcendental and worldly, may be obtained by the pilgrims who visit it. Pilgrimages are collective rituals that carry people closer to God through physical movement, which in turn symbolizes the devotees' progress toward unity with the divine. To climb Mount Kailasa, the sacred abode of Shiva, is to tangibly experience an approaching union with Shiva. Although this is the same goal that is pursued in daily worship, pilgrimage has the advantage of conveying an experiential sense of progress.

The advent of modern communications and transportation has significantly altered pilgrimage patterns. Until recently, people usually made journeys to pilgrimage sites within their general vicinity. Now people can travel to the major sites all over India with relative safety and much greater speed. Today the most famous temples draw enormous crowds, especially during important celebrations.

Festivals

Different Hindu festivals are celebrated in different regions of India. The festivals are attached to specific deities and tied to the mythology of the gods and goddesses. This means that a celebration associated with a deity who is particularly popular in one state may not be held at all in another area where that god or goddess has no following. The advent of modern television and the social

mobility of industrial urbanization is, however, creating more uni-
formity in festival observance. The following are some of the more
ubiquitous celebrations.

Among devotees of Shiva, Shivaratri is the principal celebration.
It commemorates the time Shiva appeared to a hunter who bathed a
Shiva *lingam*. During this celebration, the temple *lingam* is decorated
and people fast during the day and make offerings to Shiva. At mid-
night the fast is broken, and the following day is one of rejoicing.
Navaratri, the "nine nights," is a harvest festival devoted to the
Goddess in her different forms. People decorate the means of their
livelihoods, their taxis, cows, and office equipment, etc., and do *puja*
to them. The climax is a great *puja* to the Goddess in the form of
Durga (although she is often accompanied by images of Sarasvati
and Lakshmi). The day after Navaratri is Dassera, the celebration of
Lord Rama's victory over the demon Ravana, an incident recounted
in the famous Indian epic the *Ramayana*. This story has become popular all over India, and the Dassera festival, which celebrates the cli-
mactic battle from the text, usually includes dramatic performances
of the adventures of Rama. When a mini-series version of the
Ramayana aired on Indian television, the entire country stopped
work to watch it. In the fall, the festival of Divali, the "feast of
lights," honors Lakshmi, the goddess of good fortune. People light
small lamps and set them up in homes, at temples, or float them
down rivers, all to welcome the goddess into their homes. In this
celebration the household comes together to seek the beneficence of
Lakshmi for the whole family. The birthday of Krishna is also a time
of celebration all over India. His birth is celebrated at midnight after
a day of fasting.

Many celebrations still remain confined to specific regions. Rakhi
Day, in August, is a northern tradition. Women tie bracelets (*rakhis*)
on their brothers' wrists and pray for their health and long life, while
the brothers in turn pledge to look out for the welfare of their sisters.
If a girl has no brother, she ties the *rakhi* on the wrist of a surrogate,
perhaps a cousin, a neighbor, or a family friend. One of the most
boisterous festivals is Holi. This celebration has the air of a carnival,
as people splash each other with colored water. According to the legend that explains the origins of Holi, there was once a demoness
called Holika who ate a child every day. One day a monk suggested
that all the people gather together and meet the demoness with a
barrage of insults and abuse. As a result, Holika died of shame and
anger. Traditionally, Holi is a day when social roles are set aside, and
people may fling insults at each other with impunity.

In modern times, some Hindus have expressed concern that the festivals are becoming secular celebrations and are being dissociated from their religious roots. Watching movies and dance performances often replaces the traditional night-long singing of devotional songs. The legends behind the festivals are being forgotten in the new emphasis on festivity. The making of holy images, for instance, has become an industry, no longer the reverent craft of a few trained artisans. Neon lights and electronic images of the deities are replacing the traditional painted clay. Household festivals like Divali are becoming social events with fairs and fireworks, and sisters who live far from home may send *rakhi*s to their brothers through the mail. Nevertheless, others argue that the true spirit of the festivals is one of communal celebration, and this is still retained in the modern enthusiasm, even if the older forms are being replaced.

Hindus in California

A few Hindus came to California with the Sikh immigrants in the early part of the twentieth century. Some, who worked in agriculture, were members of the Punjabi regional culture, and others were businessmen and students who lived in urban areas. They did not establish religious organizations, although they did take part in the cultural and social gatherings of their countrymen. As single men, these first Hindu immigrants had little interest in religion. The bonds that tied them to their fellow Indians were based on culture and a shared experience in a foreign land, not faith. The Hindustani Welfare Reform Society in the Imperial Valley, for example, was formed in 1918 to aid all Indians. It fulfilled that function until the Indian community fractured along religious lines in 1948, when the Sikhs established a *gurdwara* and the Muslims formed their own Pakistan Club. Another pan-Indian organization in California was the Ghadar Party, which formed in San Francisco in 1913 to garner support for the independence movement in India. Although the party relied on Punjabi Sikhs for financial support, it was founded by a Hindu, and most of the early leaders were urban-dwelling Hindus. These early organizations were, however, primarily ethnic, cultural groups, not religious bodies, because economics and politics were the dominant concerns of the early Indian immigrants. Even when the first Hindu temple in America was built in San Francisco by the Vedanta Society in 1913, very few Asians took part in the services.

After 1946, when the immigration laws were changed to allow a

quota of one hundred Indians into the country each year and to per-
mit the reconstitution of families, the number of Hindus in California began to increase slowly. Some of these new immigrants were
students who chose to remain in America after completing their
degrees. Others were professionals seeking employment opportunities. The majority of these new immigrants came from urban,
middle-class backgrounds and moved into similar positions in
American society. A small portion of this new migratory wave was
composed of unskilled workers, especially among the Indians who
were arriving from intermediate countries in Asia and Africa, and
they also settled in cities when they reached California. It seems that
the new immigrants, mostly Hindu with some Muslims and
Christians, did not have any ties to the Punjabi culture or Sikh religion of the Indians who had taken up agricultural pursuits in the
central valleys of California. Consequently, they made no attempt to
join the rural communities but instead settled in urban areas which
offered diverse economic opportunities.

Unlike the Punjabi Sikhs, these Hindu Indians did not arrive in
groups with shared kinship or village affiliations. They came from a
wide variety of regional-linguistic cultures and had few long-term
aquaintances among their fellow immigrants. Because they were
widely scattered and isolated from their compatriots, they had little
support for religious practices, and what religion was practiced was
mostly private. Furthermore, transplanting Hinduism to a new land
proved to be a difficult task. California lacked all the elements that
make Hinduism part of the life and landscape in India. There were
no priests to perform life rituals or preside over festivals, no shrines
or temples marking places where deities had revealed themselves to
their devotees, no pilgrimage sites where famous saints had attained
enlightenment and passed on their experiences to their disciples.
For these newly arrived Hindus, whose first concern was economic
survival in a strange land, religious practice was reduced to personal prayers, meditation, and the occasional gathering of a small
group to sing devotional hymns.

In the 1950s, a small community of Gujaratis, that is, people
from the northwestern coast of India, formed in San Francisco. They
were an unusual migrant community because, unlike most of the
South Asians arriving in California at the time, they were from the
same agricultural area and knew each other before their arrival. This
community of twenty-two families created their own subculture in
the Mission district of San Francisco. They went into the hotel and
motel business, and were extraordinarily successful, as the price of

real estate increased dramatically in the 1970s. The hotel business suited them in several ways: the Gujaratis preferred to be self-sufficient rather than to work for others; they could house their families in the hotels, so they saved the cost of rent; the family could help run the hotel; and in times of trouble, such as illnesses, the extended family could help keep the business functioning. Furthermore, the hotel business helped in the reconstitution of the extended family because it provided the job-security required to sponsor the immigration of relatives. A hotelier's relatives would come to California, work in the hotel until they had learned the business, then set up their own establishments with a loan from their sponsors. In this way, the family cohesion of the San Francisco Gujarati community remained intact as it grew.

In spite of family and community ties and the shared regional-linguistic culture of Gujarat, this Indian community did not share a common religious tradition. Although most of the families were Hindus, they did not all belong to the same sect. Several families were Kabir Panthis, followers of the fifteenth-century poet-saint Kabir, who had completely rejected the idea that God could have any physical form or belong to any one religion, and who placed great emphasis on devotion as the most important aspect of religious life. Most of the other families were devotees of Vishnu who worshipped God in the forms of his various incarnations, such as Rama and Krishna. There were also several followers of the non-Hindu Jain tradition and four families who really did not think of themselves as following any particular tradition. Except for the Jains, however, none of these families evidenced strong commitments to their various religious faiths. Some of the women said prayers for their families on occasion, but not on a daily basis. Moreover, the men were not interested in religious practices at all, and there was no real effort to educate the children about Hinduism. The annual festivals, some of which traditionally involved periods of fasting and visits to temples, were treated as times for communal feasting.

The Gujaratis gave several reasons for this lack of interest in Hindu religion. The men were more interested in establishing their businesses and providing security for their families than in religious issues. In this they were acting in complete accord with Indian ideas about duty during the different stages of one's life. According to tradition, a man in the householder stage of life should marry, have children, and work hard to gain the material success necessary for the well-being of his family. He should also care for his parents, who at that point in the man's life would be retiring from active life and devoting their time to their grandchildren and to more spiritual matters. Only after a man's children are grown, married, and self-sufficient is he supposed to make religious matters his primary focus. Most of these Gujarati men hoped to be able to retire to India in comfort in their old age, after their children were educated and had become successful in their own right. The reason they gave for their desire to return to India—that American culture was too concerned with material goods and India was more spiritual—suggests that the ideal of turning one's attention toward religious pursuits in old age was still part of their ideal life pattern.

This same ideal of concern with religion in old age may explain why there was so little interest in educating the children about Hinduism. In the Indian extended family, that would normally be the job of the grandparents. Traditionally, the old folks would take their grandchildren to the local temple and tell them religious stories. Without this senior generation, however, this exchange of information was absent for the children growing up in California. The lack of temples and religious functionaries also created a problem. Without priests to perform rituals and temples to visit, the religious festivals lost much of their meaning. In India, every village has local shrines both to great deities and small local divinities that remind people of the connection between daily life and religion, but in America there were no roadside shrines to imbue the landscape with religiosity.

The women, like their husbands, were busy working for the material well-being of their families, and this interfered with their religious duties. In India, women are generally responsible for much of the household religion. They do daily *puja*s, making offerings to the images on the household altar for the benefit of the entire family. To perform the practices properly, one should make offerings every day, and the worshipper must maintain required states of purity. A woman cannot perform rituals during her menstrual period and must go through a purificatory bath after her period ends before she can again approach the altar. In the immigrant's nuclear family, where there were so few adults, it was not possible to perform the rituals every day, and thus most women did not try to keep up the traditional *puja* practice. But even though the women did not perform the *puja* ritual to the major gods like Vishnu, they did offer prayers to folk deities, especially those associated with the well-being of family members. If a husband or child fell ill, the mother might fast and promise to make a pilgrimage to a goddess' shrine when next she visited India. Thus, while the formal religious practices and communal rituals could not be carried out, personal religion and folk practices remained part of family life in California.

Cultural clubs provided a second venue for activities associated with traditional religion. These clubs were often formed by Indians with shared regional-cultural ties in India or in a country of residence prior to arrival in America. The Fiji Club of America, for example, was an association formed by East Indians who came to the San Francisco Bay Area by way of the Fiji Islands. During the 1950s and early 1960s, the club provided opportunities for people to get together with others who shared their cultural backgrounds. The meetings usually included pot-luck meals of traditional foods and entertainment in the form of music and dance performances. Since music and dance are both based on religion in India, these cultural activities were reminders of traditional religious values.

The majority of the immigrants on the West Coast in the 1950s and early 1960s were young, single men for whom these cultural clubs provided a sense of community and identity in a foreign land. As these men gained economic stability and began to start families, their interest in the cultural clubs dropped. For a time, the family replaced the association as the center of individual identity. The cultural associations reappeared, however, in the 1970s, when parents began to seek ways to teach their children about traditional Indian society.

1965 to present

After 1965, when the quota limits were lifted, the Asian-Indian community in California began to grow rapidly. Immigrants came from India and from Indian communities in other parts of the world, like the Caribbean and Africa, in ever-increasing numbers. These new arrivals were admitted to the United States under a different set of rules than previous migrants. The government had set up a list of criteria for determining who was eligible for immigration. Along with family members of people already established in the United States, "desirable" people were those who were trained in professional or technical fields such as medicine and engineering, or those who had large amounts of capital to invest. India, with its British-influenced school systems, was producing a surplus of highly educated professionals and businessmen who were finding few opportunities to use their skills and knowledge at home. These well-educated, middle-class urbanites made up the bulk of the new wave of immigrants. They came from cities in India and settled in

American cities. They did not form ethnic ghettos, as so many other migrants did, but preferred to buy homes in the suburbs, where their children would have access to good schools. Their proficiency in the English language and their westernized educations allowed them to move into the American middle class after very short periods of adjustment. On the whole, they have become the most financially successful immigrant ethnic group in the country.

This ability to attain middle-class status affects the way the immigrants perceive their culture in relation to the mainstream American culture. The urban, educated Indians did not go through a period of cultural assimilation before attaining middle-class status. Consequently, they do not feel any need to replace their traditional culture with that of the American majority in order to succeed in their new land. They see their own traditions as offering values appropriate to modern life, especially in their attitudes towards family cohesiveness, respect for elders, and sexual morality, yet they also consciously pick and choose from among American values, advocating those which they think are beneficial to success in the larger society, like strong work ethics and self-sufficiency. In this way, they are trying to preserve the important values of Indian traditions for the next generation while still encouraging their children to compete successfully in American society.

Of the Indians who have come to California since 1965, approximately twenty percent are Muslims and fifteen percent are Christians, but the majority are Hindus. As previously mentioned, India is a land of regional diversity, and these Hindu immigrants came from all over India, speaking different languages, eating different foods, and worshipping different forms of God in different rituals. Yet they shared a sense of identity as an immigrant group from a particular country with a common experience in their new land. In their first years in America, religion was not a priority for them. They were more concerned with establishing businesses and gaining security. As they began to have families, a growing need to preserve and share their heritage and religious values with their children inspired the formation of cultural groups and, eventually, the building of Hindu temples in the United States.

The first of these cultural group meetings were held in private homes, then buildings were rented or purchased to serve as community centers. Indian associations sponsored speakers from India and showed Indian films at Mexican-American theaters. These events were ecumenical gatherings that transcended regional and sectarian divisions and brought all South Asians together. Especially in the

1970s, when the migrant community was still fairly small, there was a great sense of shared Indian identity that superseded the regional-linguistic divisions of the immigrants. As one Gujarati woman said before going to see a Bengali film, "I will not understand the words, but it will be something Indian."

Hinduism became part of this Indian identity. South Asian Muslims and Christians belonged to transnational religions. Although they might have preferences for foods and music that were part of Indian culture, they could go outside the East Indian community to join other members of their faiths in religious services. Hinduism, on the other hand, was only found in South and Southeast Asia and, hence, many of the overseas Indian immigrants came to perceive it as the *de facto* religion of ethnic India. Hindus living in western countries established religious associations as a way to emphasize their cultural identity. The activities of these associations served as an integrating and cohesive force in the community. They helped the immigrants define themselves as ethnic and religious social groups, distinct from the larger American society. They also provided a way to recreate and recover some of the religious and cultural values that seemed to have been lost in the process of emigration.

Many of the religious centers in California have fostered a deliberately ecumenical spirit, trying to address the needs of all Hindus regardless of sectarian or linguistic affiliation. The first temples were established in converted buildings, often old churches purchased for this purpose. Unlike the temples in India, which have one presiding deity, the California temples housed images for all the sects that were part of their local community. As the number of Indians has grown, religion has taken on more traditional forms. In Southern California, for example, the Hindu community joined together and raised the money to build an authentic Indian temple in the hills of Malibu. The Shree Venkateswara Swami Temple, which was consecrated on May 13, 1984, is in the South Indian style, with a large ornate entry gate and separate inner shrines for each deity. It gleams pristine and white, in solitary splendor among the golden hills near Calabasas. The remoteness of the location makes it necessary for the Hindus living in the Los Angeles basin to travel an average of fifty miles to visit this temple, but also means that it has no immediate neighbors to be inconvenienced by noise or large numbers of cars.

Here, ecumenical efforts merge with traditionalism. In order to meet the needs of the diverse Hindus in Southern California, Shree

Venkateswara Temple has two areas, one devoted to Vishnu and the other to Shiva. The temple was built by traditionally trained temple craftsmen brought over from India, and the nine images it houses were crafted from granite and white marble in India. The architecture, however, was modified to meet local rulings about seismic safety and includes a multi-purpose hall and kitchen that would not be found in temples in India. There are three full-time priests who came from India on permanent visas as "ministers of religion." Although the priests perform daily rituals, the temple practices have been adapted to the new cultural environment. Special services are held on weekends so people who have to travel long distances may attend. Even the major festivals, which vary from year to year because they are calculated according to a lunar calendar, will have their culminating celebrations on weekends.

The temple was conceived as both a religious and cultural center in order to help create a sense of community for the Hindus in Southern California. It serves to preserve the socio-cultural identity of the Indian Hindu community and helps them pass on their ideals, values, cultural traditions, and moral values to their children. Along with traditional religious rituals, it is a forum for Indian music and dance performances. Children are encouraged to take classes in Indian performing arts and languages and to learn about their cultural heritage. The emphasis on music and dance as ways to teach culture may reflect a perception that rock and roll and co-ed partying are the main problems in American teen culture. Asian-Indians are particularly concerned about how American life will affect their children, especially in areas such as respect for parental authority, too much male-female social interaction, and issues surrounding traditional arranged marriages. In an effort to combat American influences, the Hindus have added a residential summer camp for the children at the temple. The camp provides a religious and cultural curriculum specifically tailored to educate children raised in the United States about their ancestral traditions. They also want to add a library that will facilitate education about the religion and culture of India.

In Northern California, the Shiva-Vishnu Temple goes even farther in its efforts to appeal to all Hindus. The temple was built with two wings that juxtapose the major architectural styles of northern and southern India. This was the result of close cooperation between the North and South Indian communities, a type of unity rarely experienced back in India. The interior of the temple also adheres to traditional forms of the two styles. In the Northern section of the temple, the images are white marble, and in the Southern section, they are carved from black granite.

These temples and centers add a communal and public element to the Hindu traditions in California. A family may perform *puja* at a family shrine and people may gather together to sing devotional songs, but if they wish to hold the large festivals and perform services for a temple image, this requires a professionally trained priest. The Hindu *samskara*s, for example, the traditional rites of passage, should be performed at the temples. These include marriage and name-giving rituals for infants. The temples are authorized to perform legal weddings and issue marriage certificates. The *samskara* rituals are held at auspicious times designated by the priests and usually include a *puja* and a *homa* (a fire ceremony). People may also request that the priest perform an *archana*, a special short *puja*, for the individual. The *archana* is a way to ask God for something important such as success in school or a business venture; or it may be a way to give thanks for good fortune.

Smaller temples, which have been established throughout the state, are less noticeable because they are not as architecturally distinct. A recent dispute arose in the city of Norwalk when the city planners rejected a proposed Hindu temple, largely because they felt it clashed with the architectural styles of the community. After much discussion, the plans for the temple were revised, and the new model calls for a mission-style building, complete with stucco walls and a red-tile roof. The size of the proposed building has also been cut back to allow for construction of more parking spaces to meet neighborhood concerns about traffic and parking. Some members of the Hindu community are not pleased with the deviation from traditional style, because temple architecture should be based on traditional ideas about sacred space, but most are more concerned with having a place to worship and offer prayers near their homes.

Despite the efforts to meet the needs of all Hindus, the earlier ecumenical centers are giving way to more specialized organizations. As the number of Indians in California has increased, from 60,000 in 1980 to 160,000 in 1990, there has been more diffraction into sub-groups. A number of Gujaratis, especially, have separated themselves from other Indians, focusing on the Swaminarayan sect, since it is a religious movement which links Gujarati cultural and religious identities. In India, the growth of this movement, which began in the nineteenth century, is centered in the state of Gujarat, and in the United States it is a growing force among Gujarati immigrants. The spread of the movement is being facilitated by a desire to take part in the cultural milieu of the homeland. The use of the Vedas and *Bhagavadgita* as sacred texts, devotion to Krishna, and adherence to rituals like *puja* mark the Swaminarayan tradition as part of mainstream Hinduism, but the language, architecture, iconography, calendar, cuisine, and dress adopted by this group are common only to Gujarat. Gatherings include meals of Gujarati food and fellowship with others who speak the same language. No other group has worked harder to teach their children the old-world language and culture in order to preserve and pass on their traditions. The exclusivity of this community facilitates the preservation of its culture. There is no need to find ways to meet the needs of devotees of different gods or speakers of different languages as in the ecumenical temples. Like the Punjabi Sikhs, the Gujarati Swaminarayans have been able to create their own cultural sub-group within America.

Many smaller sects have gradually broken away from the large, ecumenical temple associations to build their own religious centers. One of the newest is the Shree Ramkabir temple in Carson, thirty miles from Los Angeles. The founders hope this temple will be a place of harmony for all people because it is dedicated to the fifteenth century poet-saint Kabir, who rejected all sectarian and religious divisions. Kabir also stressed knowledge and devotion and taught that rituals performed without understanding were useless and ideas about the superiority of one religion with a particular name for God were blind folly. The Kabir followers who support this new California temple—the first memorial to Kabir outside India—hope their belief that there is only one God, whether called Ram or Christ, will help Indians put aside the divisions that are developing along sectarian lines and recover a sense of communal harmony. Thus the temple is to be a center for social and educational interaction rather than religious congregation. The worship offered there will be less formal than the ritualized ceremonies of *brahmin* priests at other temples.

Annual festivals honoring the Hindu deities offer opportunities for different religious groups to join together. In 1988, twenty Hindu organizations in the San Francisco Bay Area joined together to celebrate the culmination of the festivities associated with the birthday of Ganesha, the elephant-headed god. Ganesha is the remover of obstacles and is honored at the beginning of a new task. Images of this deity are often placed over the doorway of a home. Although most Indians are familiar with the genial elephant god, the annual

Ganesha celebration is a tradition that comes primarily from the state of Maharashtra on the west coast of India. During these celebrations, the Hindus set up clay images of the elephant-headed god in their religious centers, and the deity is invoked to become present in the images so his devotees may have the opportunity to make offerings to him. The last day of the festival marks the departure of Ganesha, when the images are dissolved in the ocean, signifying Ganesha's return to all-pervasive consciousness. The Hindus who gathered at Baker Beach in San Francisco performed *puja* (made offerings) to each image, enjoyed a cultural program and a festive lunch, and then carried the images down into the ocean.

The ocean which received the Ganesha images is the same body of water that bathes the shores of Asia, but establishing Hinduism on the land that borders the opposite side of the Pacific has not been easy. Hindu ritual practices sometimes clash with suburban California etiquette. The large gatherings that mark major festivals have occasionally created problems for Hindu temples in residential neighborhoods. The residents have expressed frustration about the number of cars that jam their streets and the noise coming from the celebrations. Most of these problems have been resolved by discussion, and some temples have limited the number of festivals to be held each year. New religious centers are planning extra parking facilities to help prevent such issues from arising, but it is hard to find good temple locations. Sites like that of the large Calabasas temple, which is several miles from any residence, do not have problems with noise or traffic, but the remote location makes visits a day-long enterprise, so it is not possible for Hindus to drop by on a daily basis on their way to or from work as they would in India.

One of the greatest difficulties in transplanting Hinduism to a new world has been its strong ties to the physical land of India. Temples in India have origin stories that tell how the presiding deity revealed himself at that location, shrines mark the sites where great saints achieved enlightenment and instructed their disciples, and the rivers are goddesses whose waters wash away human impurities. In America, where the land is not part of Hindu mythology, the only holy places are the temples, which have borrowed the character of the sacred sites in India after which they are modeled. Nevertheless, the consecrated images within the temples are making the Hindu deities part of the American landscape. Slowly this new world is being sacralized for Indian immigrants. Many have noted that the Calabasas temple site has seven hills, like the site of the original Shree Venkateswara Temple in India. Moreover, the

Pacific Ocean has now received several images of Ganesha at the end of his annual celebrations, just like the ocean and rivers of India. And, in 1989, a Shiva *lingam* appeared in Golden Gate Park.

The story of the Golden Gate Park *lingam* is interesting and reveals the depth of the Indian sacralization process. The *lingam* appeared at a crossroads of three footpaths among the stones of a disassembled sixteenth-century Christian monastery. After a few Hindus noticed the stone, word spread, and people began to visit to make offerings of flowers and fruit. Folk from the Shakti Mandir (temple) in San Francisco soon began to observe a regular worship service in the park, and gradually the stone came to be covered with sandalwood paste and adorned with garlands of flowers. The *lingam* became a place of pilgrimage for Hindus in the Bay Area. As it turns out, the lingam was originally a bollard, or street barrier, which the city had abandoned in the park. Recognizing that it had religious significance, the city helped move the stone to a private location because religious sites are not allowed on city property.

Another problem for Hindus in California has been the absence of holy men and women. In India, wandering monks are an everyday sight, naked ascetics practice *yoga* on the riverbanks, and festival processions draw crowds of renunciates from diverse sects to fill the streets. Such monks are not, however, part of the immigrant community. Here in California, the most visible religious figures have been the temple priests and a few visiting monks who come on sponsored tours to give lectures. This may soon change. In 1992, the U.S. Congress loosened the qualifications that defined "religious workers" for immigration purposes and added a new "lay religious worker" category. Previously only priests were qualified for immigration, although successful arguments had been made for a few monks. Now immigration is open to religious teachers, temple craftsmen, counselors, and missionaries. There may soon be more Hindus like Guru Narayanaya, who resides at a small *ashram* in Garden Grove. His followers come and go without appointments, asking advice in daily matters and listening to his wisdom. He is like the wise men of traditional village India, a humble renunciate who lives a life devoted to God and shares his knowledge with those who seek him out.

Although much time and effort has been expended in the temples for the purpose of sharing the Hindu faith with children growing up in America, the second generation has not absorbed the religious traditions in the same way their parents did. For the children, Hinduism has largely been a matter of Sunday school classes and weekend festivals, rather than everyday practices. Often their parents have found it a struggle to define Hinduism for their children. To be Hindu in India was simply to take part in the rituals and festivals that permeated the mainstream culture. It is this bond between culture and religion that explains the importance Hindu parents attach to teaching their religious heritage to the next generation. The real purpose of religious education among California Hindus is not to teach children the names of a few deities, but to pass on to the next generation the rich cultural traditions of India, with their guiding principles for leading a moral life. In other words, to teach Hindu *dharma* (virtuous living). Parents see their Indian value system as offering much that is lacking in American culture; they stress the importance of their traditional emphases on family, morality, and respect for elders. Sociologists theorize that an ethnic group that is able to succeed in a foreign country without cultural assimilation will feel no need to abandon its old ways. Indians, with their high levels of education and English proficiency, have been able to move into the American middle class without assimilation. They have not felt the need to abandon their natal culture in order to adapt to their new environment. Instead, they have created a dichotomy between home and work, whereby they follow traditional patterns at home and American patterns at work. Religion is part of the traditional life associated with home and the cultural community.

This dichotomy may be more difficult for the second generation. They spend a great deal of time in the mainstream American culture at school, where they absorb American lifestyles. These affect relations between generations. For example, second-generation Indian Americans rarely maintain vegetarian diets, even though vegetarianism has become a symbol of adherence to traditional values within the immigrant community. It is harder to buck peer pressure than to break with traditional behavior.

The greatest stress, however, seems to come from traditional expectations about proper gender-related behavior and arranged marriages. Young women, in particular, are under pressure to follow restrictive rules of behavior. Because they live in America, there is a fear that they will be "corrupted" and have loose morals. If they dress in western clothing and wear make-up, people might assume they are not well-behaved, dutiful daughters. Indian-American women often complain that they are more restricted than their counterparts back in India because their association with the U.S. makes them suspect even if they behave perfectly.

The object of these behavioral restrictions is, of course, to ensure eligibility for a good marriage. Marriages have traditionally been arranged by the parents. Often American parents prefer to select a bride from India for their son, assuming such a woman will be well versed in the traditional duties of a wife and daughter-in-law. In spite of this preference, American women generally do not lack for prospective mates, because Indian men who marry them automatically become eligible for citizenship. Unfortunately, many of these matches between Americanized Indians and new immigrants are troubled. The young couples do not share common experiences or expectations of how to carry out their new family roles because they have grown up in different cultures. Unions between couples who have shared the common experience of growing up in an Asian-American household are much more successful. These marriages are becoming more common as parents, bowing to the realities of changed circumstances, give their children more voice in the selection of a prospective spouse.

The second-generation Hindus in California are slowly finding their own balance between their parents' traditions and their modern American experiences. Growing up with a religion that is separated from its cultural milieu, the second generation has shown a tendency to reject ideas that clash with western ideals. These Indian Americans are developing an interpretation of the Hindu tradition that is mostly in alignment with the modern reform and renewal movements that began in India as early as the eighteenth century and have been called Neo-Hinduism. Neo-Hindu movements claim to have recovered the original core teachings of Hindu spirituality as they were recorded in the Upanishads (ca. 900–500 B.C.E.), while ridding themselves of corruptions and degenerations like caste divisions and useless rituals. They describe the message of Hinduism as the essence of all true spirituality, and thus equivalent to the essence of all religious traditions. These American Hindus shy away from the idolatrous implications of worshipping temple images and prefer to describe God as dwelling within people. Many of them do not accept the idea of reincarnation and have no desire to understand the purpose of most of the rituals performed at the temples. Furthermore, they do not place any reliance on the efficacy of the old folk traditions like promising to make a pilgrimage in order to gain the favor of a deity.

Yet these young Indian Americans are proud of their cultural heritage and firm in their desire to retain an Indian identity. They actively help their parents organize youth camps where they can learn about their ancestral traditions. These meetings provide a forum for communication between generations and help make sense out of the religious practices. They also give the children a chance to spend time in the company of other Hindus, where they feel normal and accepted. Teenagers who express dismay at the seeming oddity of their parents' beliefs in a multitude of gods and goddesses gain new appreciation for Hinduism when they hear people their own age talk about mystical experiences in which they have seen visions of Rama and his wife, Sita. When the testimonials come from their peers, they gain credence. East Indians are also taking advantage of courses in religion offered at their colleges in order to learn more about their ancestral traditions.

To this second generation, Hinduism is often more a part of their cultural identity than part of a genuine spirituality. Interestingly, most of these American-raised Hindus define themselves as Indians, not Gujaratis or Bengalis, and criticize the growing regional and caste differentiation among their parents. Some young folks have expressed the hope that their generation, with its shared American experiences and exposure to diverse cultures, will be able to transcend these prejudices. The unified identity of the second generation bodes well for the development of a truly American Hindu tradition, especially if these young people start to feel a greater interest in religion as they start to have families of their own.

Bibliography

Bhardwaj, S.M. "Hindu Deities and Pilgrimage in the United States." In *Pilgrimage in the United States*. Berlin: Dietrich Reimer Verlag, 1990.

Dasgupta, Sathi S. *On the Trail of an Uncertain Dream: Indian Immigrant Experience in America*. New York: AMS Press, Inc., 1989.

Fenton, John Y. *Transplanting Religious Traditions: Asian Indians in America*. New York: Praeger Publishers, 1988.

Fuller, C. J. *The Camphor Flame: Popular Hinduism and Society in India*. Princeton: Princeton University Press, 1992.

Hinduism Today. Published by the Himalayan Academy. San Francisco, California.

Hopkins, Thomas J. *The Hindu Religious Tradition*. Belmont: Wadsworth Publishing Company, 1971.

India Today, North American Special Supplement.

Jain, Usha R. *The Gujaratis of San Francisco*. New York: AMS Press, Inc., 1989

Jaini, Padmanabh S. *The Jaina Path of Purification*. Berkeley: University of California Press, 1979.

Klostermaier, Klaus K. *A Survey of Hinduism*. New York: State University of New York Press, 1989.

Melton, J. Gordon, editor. *The Encyclopedia of American Religions*. Third Edition. Detroit: Gale Research Inc., 1989.

Ong, Paul, Bonacich, Edna, and Cheng Lucie, editors. *The New Asian Immigration in Los Angeles and Global Restructuring*. Philadelphia: Temple University Press, 1994.

Richardson, E. Allen. *East Comes West: Asian Religions and Cultures in North America*. New York: The Pilgrim Press, 1985.

Shankar, Richard Ashok Kumar. *The East Indians of the Greater San Francisco Bay Area of California: A Study of an Ethnic-Status Community*. Dissertation: Boston College, 1976.

Williams, Raymond Brady. *Religions of Immigrants from India and Pakistan: New Threads in the American Tapestry*. Cambridge: Cambridge University Press, 1988.

Williams, Raymond Brady, editor. *A Sacred Thread: Modern Transmission of Hindu Traditions in India and Abroad*. Chambersburg: Anima Publications, 1992.

4 Buddhists: Refugees and Missionaries

On Saturday mornings, the early morning sun shines down on the orange robes of a procession of Buddhist monks walking through a residential neighborhood in North Hollywood. In single file, the monks proceed from the Wat Thai temple to the front yards of about a dozen Thai American families who offer them food and water. Making such rounds is part of daily monastic life in Asia—it helps the monks rid themselves of material desires and allows the community to improve its spiritual state by supporting the monks. In California, the procession has become a symbolic means to affirm the importance of Buddhism in daily life.

Buddhism

The Buddhist tradition that developed around the preaching of a wandering teacher named Gautama Siddhartha from the sixth century before the Common Era did not stay in India. Buddhist monks carried their teacher's message down to Sri Lanka, east into Asia, and north into the Himalayas. Over the years, doctrinal changes inspired the emergence of several different schools, and the faith was adapted to different cultural milieus. But all Buddhists share the basic teachings attributed to the Buddha, and all recite the threefold "refuge": "I take refuge in the Buddha, I take refuge in the Dhamma, I take refuge in the Sangha."

The Buddha

The founder of Buddhism was probably the son of a chief of the Shakya hill-tribe from north of the Gangetic plain. Before he achieved enlightenment, the Buddha ("the enlightened one") was known as Gautama Siddhartha. According to tradition, as a young

77

man he left his family to pursue religious enlightenment, and after years of study and trying different paths, he attained his goal. He then turned to teaching others to follow a Middle Way between extreme asceticism and worldy life. Many of the stories and teachings preserved in the Buddhist texts must have been added long after Gautama's life, but it is clear that there was such a teacher who came from the Shakya clan, that he achieved enlightenment under a tree at Gaya, that he became a teacher and organized a band of followers, and finally died at the age of about eighty. According to Sri Lankan tradition, Gautama lived from 624 to 544 B.C.E., but most western scholars now place his lifespan from 563 to 483. After the Buddha's death, his cremated remains were distributed to various centers and interred in *stupas*. The earliest *stupas* were simple mounds that served as places of homage. Gradually they became more elaborate, and were covered with brick, stone, plaster, and even precious metals. Today, *stupas* holding relics of revered Buddhist monks are still prominent, alone or as part of a temple.

The early Buddhists emphasized the humanity of their teacher. He was a mortal man who had achieved enlightenment, and thus he served as a model for others seeking to escape from the cycle of rebirth. Moreover, because of his personal attainment, he was able to perceive the true nature of human existence and tell others the best path to realize that same knowledge for themselves. Early Buddhist art never depicted Gautama because the Buddha had attained final *nirvana*, total freedom from the cycle of rebirth, and therefore he no longer existed as an individual who could be represented. Unlike the gods, who could be depicted because they continued to reside in a heavenly realm, he had ceased to exist. So the monks used symbols to show that the Buddha had been in the world to teach people, although he was no longer present. Among these symbols were footprints, a chair with a depression in its cushion, or the tree under which he had attained enlightenment.

Gradually, as a feeling of more personal devotion to the Buddha developed in tandem with the rise of *bhakti* (devotional) traditions in Hinduism, images from the mythology of the Buddha's lives appeared. By the first century B.C.E., statues of the Buddha were popular. He was usually represented in one of three postures, lying, sitting, or standing. Most temples now have images, but these are not embodiments of the living presence of the Buddha, like the deities in the Hindu temples; rather they are reminders of the historical teacher who came to spread his Dhamma, his knowledge and path, in order to aid people who were caught in the cycle of rebirth.

The Dhamma

The teachings of the Buddha are called the Dharma in Sanskrit or Dhamma in the Pali language which was first used to write them down. The Buddha taught that there are Four Noble Truths. One, all life is characterized by suffering. Two, this suffering is the result of attachment to and desire for things in a world that is impermanent and always changing. Three, it is possible to completely stop these desires and be free of these attachments. Four, the way to achieve this freedom is to follow the Eightfold Path taught by the Buddha: right views, right aspirations, right speech, right conduct, right livelihood, right effort, right attentiveness, and right concentration. This path constitutes a way of living. The first three involve accepting the Four Noble Truths and Buddhist ideas about the nature of the self, determining to live in accord with Buddhist teachings, and avoiding falsehood or harmful speech. Right conduct means living a moral life and following the five Buddhist vows to abstain from taking life, stealing, lying, adultery, or drinking intoxicants. Right livelihood requires one to avoid vocations that compromise Buddhist teachings, for example being a butcher or a soldier. Right effort means working to develop charity, compassion, and humility. Right mindfulness involves disciplined control of mind and body, and right concentration describes advanced meditation leading to the highest wisdom, peace, and freedom from rebirth. All Buddhists are encouraged to follow the first three steps, but the others are more easily engaged in as a member of the monastic community.

Central to the Buddha's teachings is his doctrine of impermanence. Life, according to the Buddha, is a stream of becoming. There is nothing permanent in the empirical self, since one thing is dependent on another. One conceives of one's "self" as a composite of perceptions, feelings, motivations, intelligence, and form. But these are constantly changing, and when the individual dies, these all cease to exist. Since, according to the Buddha, all the aspects that make up the self are transient, he questioned the Hindu belief in a permanent unchanging self that enters the body at birth and leaves it at death. The Buddha replaced the Hindu theory of an eternal self with the "no-soul" or "no-self" doctrine.

Instead of a transmigrating self in a physical body, the Buddha described the individual as an aggregate of body, sensation, perception, predisposition, and consciousness. All of these change over a lifetime and cease to form a cohesive whole when one dies. But *karma* survives after the falling away of the five aggregates. *Karma*, the law of causation, operates to assemble another five aggregates, which constitute a new individual who will continue on the trajectory laid down by the actions of the previous life. This new being is thus conditioned by the old being, without being identical to it.

This cycle of rebirth goes on until the individual realizes that the aggregates of the empirical self are not really a permanent self. Because of our ignorance and selfishness, we do not see the true nature of our selves. When we get rid of this ignorance, we attain *nirvana*, which is described negatively as freedom from ignorance, selfishness, and suffering, and positively as the attainment of wisdom, compassion, and a state of peace where there are no desires. *Nirvana* can only be achieved by self-effort. There is no savior deity in Buddhism. The gods who make their way into Buddhist theology are described as residing in a heavenly realm, but they too are caught up in the cycle of rebirth. If one leads a meritorious life, one may be reborn as a god in heaven for a time. Then when the merit is exhausted, one returns to earth once again. Indeed, human birth is more desirable than divine life because only people have the opportunity to hear the Buddha's teachings and follow his instructions until they finally break the cycle of rebirth.

The Sangha

During his lifetime, the Buddha organized his followers into a community called the Sangha. The monks were called *bhikkhus*, "beggars," because they had to give up all possessions and live by begging. They were to follow strict rules of behavior, which included continuous movement from place to place for eight months out of the year and consumption of only one meal a day. These practices were designed to help them overcome their attachments and desires. Pious layfolk would support the monks by giving food and making donations of land for retreats. Out of this, settled monastic communities developed. The monks and nuns were able to devote their lives to meditation and self-discipline, but remained in contact with the laity through the tradition of begging. Monks and layfolk were thus bound together: the monks expounded the teaching and provided an example of saintly living, while the laity sustained their efforts with food and shelter.

Buddhism, especially in its early years, focused on monastic life and those practices which would help the monks and nuns gain the self-mastery necessary to attain true knowledge and *nirvana*. Lay Buddhists tried to live according to the same precepts of behavior, but only monks had the necessary time to practice the physical and mental discipline necessary for the attainment of *nirvana*. Moreover, monks were required to observe a code of discipline in their daily lives that was nearly impossible to maintain outside a monastery. The primary focus of monastic life was study and meditation. The main responsibility to the public was to teach those who came for instruction. As monastic life became more elaborate, a new dimension of public ceremony emerged. Monks came to serve as temple priests, performing public ceremonies and leading chants, but the few life-cycle rituals that have developed, such as marriages and funerals, are purely local traditions.

The laity were essential to the continuation of the Buddhist community, since they supported the temples. Although the Buddha did not think it would be possible for layfolk to attain *nirvana*, because daily responsibilities would prevent them from spending the necessary time in meditation, nevertheless they could gain better rebirths by living meritorious lives. Then, in these next lives they would be able to reach the final goal. One of the best ways to gain merit was, of course, by supporting the Sangha. Layfolk might also spend some time in the monastery studying and meditating.

In modern times, the relation between monks and laity has grown closer. Layfolk may become disciples of particular Buddhist teachers and in some sects there is "lay ordination," in which a senior disciple is allowed to carry out priestly functions such as leading services. These disciples are treated as members of the Sangha, even if they do not live in the temple or monastery.

The Turnings of the Wheel of Dhamma

There are three major types of Buddhism, sometimes referred to as the "three turnings" of the Wheel of Dhamma. Of course, this term is used by members of the third group to show that theirs is the final form of Buddhism, but it also acknowledges that all three traditions are based on the Buddha's Dhamma. These three traditions are Theravada, Mahayana, and Vajrayana Buddhism. The division into Theravada and Mahayana schools was well established by the second century C.E., and Vajrayana Buddhism emerged out of the Mahayana tradition around the sixth century and prospered during the eighth century.

Theravada Buddhism, "the path of the elders," is closely tied to the textual tradition preserved in the Pali Canon, the collection of teachings attributed to the Buddha and his earliest disciples and commentaries on those teachings. The Theravada tradition places great emphasis on the importance of monastic life and adhering to the rules laid out by the Buddha. The goal of existence is defined as *nirvana*, and the ideal toward which Buddhists should strive is the *arhat*, the "saint," who frees himself from the bondage of *karma* by his own efforts. Generally, it is thought that only monks are able to devote enough time to study of scripture and meditation to achieve these goals. Although the Buddha serves as a model of what others may attain, it is important to emphasize that he does not serve the function of a savior god in Theravada Buddhism. The Theravadins believe that self-effort is the way to attain their goals, not divine grace. There has been worship of the Buddha, but this served as an act of commemoration, not a petition for grace. Even when local popular deities worked their way into Buddhism, they served as objects of meditation, not as ultimate divinities.

The Mahayana tradition places more emphasis on later commentaries than on the Pali Canon, arguing that the Pali texts were for ignorant people who were not yet ready to understand the real spirit of the Buddha's teachings. In Mahayana, the historical teacher is just one aspect of the transcendent, eternal Buddha. This is explained as the *trikaya* or "three-body" doctrine, which describes the Buddha as existing on three different levels and in three corresponding forms or bodies. The first of the Buddha's bodies is the physical person who was born into the world and lived out a normal human life. But this was just a temporary body, one of a series of human forms taken on in order to bring the Buddhist Dhamma to humanity. There are also a multitude of heavenly Buddhas, one for each heavenly realm, which correlate with the second body, the Body of Bliss. These ensure that the Dhamma is available throughout the cosmos. The third body is the Body of Essence or Body of Law, which is a permanent truth that exists outside the human body and connects all the Buddhas, past, present, and future, in the earthly and heavenly realms. It remains even after the physical body of the Buddha dies and is the only real body of the Buddha. Furthermore, it is eternal and all-pervasive. Since the Body of Law is all-pervasive, it is present in all sentient beings as their inner "Buddha-nature," and because of this innate Buddha-nature, all beings are capable of becoming enlightened. This enlightenment can be attained by living a life of faith and devotion to the Buddha, and showing compassion for all fellow beings. Thus, in Mahayana Buddhism, there is a shift away from complete reliance on meditation practices, as in Theravada, and a tendancy to incorporate devotional practices. In addition, the *arhat* ideal is replaced by the *bodhisattva*, the Buddha-in-the-making who, out of compassion, turns back from *nirvana* to devote himself to bringing enlightenment to all beings. Furthermore, a *bodhisattva* can share his merit with others, thereby creating a system of grace in direct contrast to the Theravada insistence on self-effort.

Vajrayana Buddhism, or Tantrism, is a branch of Mahayana that employs unique symbolism and methods to achieve enlightenment. These include the use of *mantras*, which are special utterances designed to direct the mind toward correct knowledge, performance of symbolic gestures called *mudras*, and a special meditation practice that uses visualization to identify the meditator with specific deities. These practices must be carried out under the guidance of a master who formally initiates disciples into the tradition. There are two types of Tantrism, "Left-hand" and "Right-hand." Left-hand Tantrism has been much misunderstood because it incorporates certain sexual practices into its rituals. These practices are a physical enactment of the union of wisdom and compassion. Wisdom (*prajna*), interpreted as the realization of the nonexistence of everything that appears in the phenomenal world, is perceived as female; and compassion, the urge to carry out altruistic activities to save others, is male. The Mahayana enlightenment, described as the union of wisdom and compassion, is thus depicted in Tantric iconography as the passionate embrace of a male Buddha or *bodhisattva* and his female consort. In Right-hand Tantra, on the other hand, the masculine and feminine elements are internalized as subtle energies in the human body, and hence their union is achieved through meditation practices alone.

This book has as its focus the religious traditions from South Asia, a region that includes the Buddhist countries of Sri Lanka and Tibet. Theravada Buddhism is the primary tradition in Sri Lanka and Vajrayana Buddhism is the dominant tradition of Tibet, so we will be dealing extensively with these traditions. Some data about the Theravadins of the Southeast Asian Thai, Burmese, and Cambodian communities of California will be included as well because there is considerable overlap among these Buddhists. The Mahayana tradition, which comes to California from China, Japan, and Korea, will be covered in a separate book in this series.

Theravada Buddhism

Sri Lanka

During the reign of Ashoka, when Buddhism enjoyed royal patronage in India, missionaries began taking the religion beyond the Indian subcontinent. They traveled south of India to the island of Sri Lanka (Ceylon) around 247 B.C.E., bringing Theravada Buddhism, which was predominant in India during that era. At that time, Sri Lanka was ruled by a dynasty of Indo-Aryan Sinhalese clansmen who had migrated from the Gangetic plain much earlier, bringing Brahmanical customs and political institutions to the southern island. According to tradition, their ruler, King Tissa, was converted to Buddhism by Ashoka's son and other missionaries about 247 B.C.E. The populace converted more slowly, but by the second century B.C.E., the Sinhalese were Buddhists. King Tissa encouraged the acceptance of the new religion by patronizing Buddhist missionaries and by giving the Buddhists a royal pavilion in his capital, Anuradhapura, from which to organize conversions of the royal household and the people. Next, a monastery was established, a shoot of the Bodhi Tree was brought from Bodhgaya by Ashoka's daughter (who also founded an order of nuns), and a huge *stupa* (reliquary) was constructed for popular worship.

All this established a close relationship between Buddhism and the government in Sri Lanka from the very beginning. Kings were practicing Buddhists and patrons of Buddhist art, learning, and worship. For more than 2,000 years, Theravada Buddhism was closely linked to the Sinhalese monarchy. The royal family supported the construction of shrines and monasteries, and even took a hand in the regulation of the Sangha. The same sort of patronage was practiced by the nobility. With all this support, beautiful monuments were built and monasteries became centers of culture and learning. The Buddhism of Sri Lanka has had a longer continuous heritage than that of any other country in the world.

Challenges to the Theravada tradition in Sri Lanka came from Mahayana Buddhists who arrived during the third and fourth centuries, then from Tantric teachings that were brought over in the eighth and ninth centuries, and last by Hindus from the region of Tamilnadu in South India. In the eleventh century, King Vijayabahu fought to liberate Sri Lanka from a Tamil Hindu occupation and then to revive the state religion. Hindu invasions continued to disrupt the country and endanger the Buddhist Sangha. Throughout this period, all the way up to the 1500s, land revenues declined, thereby reducing support for Buddhist institutions, and the Sangha grew weaker in spite of continued patronage by the kings and nobles. The old, great monasteries were disbanded, and schisms and lack of discipline disrupted the Sangha until the kings had to intervene in order to weed out undesirable members from the Sangha. Because of the continued Hindu influence on Sri Lankan society, the worship of Hindu gods gradually became part of popular Buddhist practice and Brahmanical deities came to be worshipped by kings and laity in elaborate festivals.

In 1505, the Portuguese seized the lowlands of Sri Lanka, destroying monasteries and forcibly converting people to Catholicism. The Portuguese remained a force in Sri Lanka until 1658. During this time, the Sinhala kings withdrew to Kandy, in the mountains, where they ruled from 1592 to 1815, supporting Buddhism as far as they were able. In spite of such efforts, the Sangha so declined in the sixteenth century that the indigenous ordination tradition, which had passed the Buddhist teachings from teacher to novice in an unbroken line for centuries, was lost; and a valid ordination tradition was not re-established until the Thai mission of 1753. The largest body of monks in Sri Lanka today, the Siyam Niyaka, traces its ordination back to the Thai visit to Kandy. The Thai tradition, however, originally derived from Sri Lanka, via Burma, so in a roundabout way the modern Sangha has maintained their cultural heritage and a succesion from teacher to novice, which can be traced back to the first Buddhist missionaries in Sri Lanka.

Dutch Calvinists and the British followed the Portuguese in controlling the island of Sri Lanka. This period of European domination further damaged the Buddhist Sangha. When the British took over the Sinhala monarchy in 1802, part of the treaty they signed bound them to protect Buddhism, but evangelical Christian missionaries moved in unhindered and attacked the local traditions. Fortunately, Buddhism rose to this challenge. New leaders emerged to form lay associations and establish training centers for monks, and there was something of a revival of Theravada Buddhism in Sri Lanka. Two Westerners aided the Buddhist cause. One was Henry Olcott, of the American Theosophical Society, who not only traveled around the island exhorting the Sri Lankans to revive their historic tradition, but also helped set up Buddhist schools as an alternative to the Western schools, which stressed Christian education. The other Westerner was T.W. Rhys Davids, the founder of the Pali Text Society. Rhys Davids' translations of Buddhist texts brought acclaim and respect for the teachings of Buddhism to the people of Europe and gave confidence and pride to the Buddhists themselves, as well as elevating their position in the eyes of their foreign associates.

In the twentieth century, Buddhists in Sri Lanka have contributed a great deal of valuable scholarship to the Buddhist world. When Sri Lanka achieved independence from foreign rule in 1948, the Buddhists once again began to take an active part in the affairs of their country and in Buddhism throughout Asia. In 1950, for example, they founded the World Fellowship of Buddhists, an effort to unite Buddhists of all nations.

Burma

Burma (now Mayanmar) was India's gateway for trade to Southeast Asia. King Ashoka sent monks as missionaries to the commercial center of Thaton, and by the second century B.C.E., the monastic settlement there was sending Burmese monks to participate in religious ceremonies in Sri Lanka. Thaton became a great Buddhist center during the years of commerce with India in the first part of the Common Era. *Stupas* were built in Burma and the general prosperity of the period supported monastic communities, where education and discipline were available for monks and laity.

Later, Mahayana influences from China, Tantrism from Bengal, and Indian Hinduism among the Cambodian Khmers began to affect Burmese Buddhism. During the eleventh century, the Burmese turned to Sri Lanka for support. A monk went to the capital city of Pagan, where he converted King Anawrahta to Theravada. With the king as a champion of the Theravada tradition, Mahayana and Tantra lost ground. Burma then became the most active center of Buddhism in the world, at a time when the tradition was under attack or failing in most other areas. The king had relics brought from Sri Lanka, and he instituted magnificent building programs in Pagan.

In 1065, when King Vijayabahu of Sri Lanka wanted to revive his country's fading Theravada tradition, monks from Burma traveled to the island to restore the ordination line. For years, Burma was the most prosperous Theravada country in the world. Even the Cambodian Khmers were eventually brought into the Buddhist fold through the efforts of the Burmese.

The Burmese Theravada tradition survived the Mongol sack of Pagan in 1287 and the succeeding period of small kingdoms and warfare. In the fifteenth century, the Burmese Sangha was reformed, and the capital again became a center of Theravada culture. The new monarchy, which ruled until the British overthrow of the king in 1886, favored the Sangha. Pali studies flourished, texts were translated into Burmese, and the king appointed a hierarchy to regulate the affairs of the Order. When the British took over, they declined to appoint a new director to this regulatory post and made the Sangha responsible for electing its own leaders. This removal of outside authority led to a deterioration in monastic discipline.

Nevertheless, the Burmese Theravada tradition survived to play a prominant part in the early independence movement and is the main religion of the country today.

Thailand and Cambodia

Indian religions and culture traveled into Southeast Asia with *brahmin* and Buddhist traders, and by the fourth century, the Cambodian area was largely Indianized. Hinduism and Mahayana Buddhism were predominant until the eleventh century. In the late twelfth century, a Burmese monk introduced Theravada Buddhism into Cambodia. Later it was supported by Khmer kings and eventually supplanted the Mahayana tradition. At the end of the thirteenth century, the state had officially replaced Hinduism with Theravada Buddhism.

In the thirteenth century, small Thai states developed on the Indo-Chinese peninsula. Influenced by Burma and the Khmers, they too adopted Theravada Buddhism. King Ramkham-haeng (twelfth–thirteenth centuries) patronized Theravada and encouraged his subjects to adopt the tradition. The spread of Buddhism was so successful that even when fifteenth-century Thai kings once again took up Brahmanical Hindu ideas, borrowed from Cambodia, Thailand remained a Buddhist country. By that time, the Sangha was responsible for education as well as religion, and people from all social classes considered themselves Buddhists. The Thai Theravadins drew support from the Sri Lankans, and as we have mentioned above, the Sri Lankan ordination line was renewed from the Thai monastic community in the eighteenth century. Theravada Buddhism remains the primary religion of Thailand to this day.

Theravada Practices

Theravada Buddhist practices have traditionally been quite different for monks and layfolk. The doctrines and practices of Theravada Buddhism are based on the Pali texts called the Tipitaka, the "three baskets." The first "basket," a group of scriptures called the *Vinaya Pitaka*, lays out a detailed code of behavior for the Sangha of monks and nuns. The daily activities of the clergy are oriented around meditation and study. The objects of study are the second and third baskets, the *Sutta Pitaka*, consisting of five collections of the Buddha's discourses, and the *Abhidhamma Pitaka*, which contains seven works presenting the Buddha's teachings. The only formal duty enjoined on monks in relation to the laity is a responsibility for preaching and instructing them in applying Buddhist val-

ues to life. Theravada Buddhism has developed a few public cere-
monials, most notably Wesak, the festival during the full moon in
May, which celebrates the birth, enlightenment, and death of the
Buddha. The clergy may be called on to perform rites for the sick
and to protect households, but mostly they serve the community by
acting as a living example to the layfolk of the higher goals of religion and by providing opportunities for the laity to earn merit
through charity toward monks and nuns.

The great monasteries of Sri Lanka were made possible by the
level of support the monks received. Although ideally the monks
and nuns were to live by begging, in pre-modern times they were
also provided for by the kings and nobility. There were periodic
attempts to reform the tradition, especially when the monks were
perceived as self-satisfied. These reform movements contributed to
the revival of forest-dwelling hermit practices by some monks. They
lived in caves or huts in the jungle, practicing strict meditation. The
nearby villages cared for them because their reputation for merit
was thought to make the villagers' offerings especially potent and
meritorious.

For the laity, traditional Theravada Buddhism has mostly involved support of the monks. Layfolk practice specific works of
piety, such as feeding clergy, sending a son or daughter into the
Order, and going to monasteries to circumambulate the *stupa*. The
poorest and the richest can give gifts to the Sangha, and all such
deeds bring merit, which may help the individual attain heaven or
at least a more favorable rebirth. The laity generally hope to attain
heaven, even though it is not a permanent residence, and they tend
to regard spiritual growth culminating in *nirvana* as a higher goal
that only monks and nuns can hope to achieve. The clergy serve as
constant reminders of the ideal of letting go of attachments and
seeking a goal beyond ordinary goals. Non-clergy often spend some
time in a monastery studying Buddhist teachings and practicing
meditation, especially around the age of twenty, when one is eligible for ordination. Usually, after a few months, or maybe one rainy
season, the individual leaves the monastery and takes up the life of
a householder. These periods of training bring merit to the monk
and to his family and serve to preserve the Buddhist teachings.

Layfolk also observe numerous practices which are not strictly
Buddhist. The images in their temples may receive offerings of fruit,
flowers, and incense, and are honored in a *puja* ritual borrowed
from Hinduism. Although the images are not considered living
embodiments of the divine presence, as in Hinduism, making offer-

ings to them is a way to gain merit and mental purification. Buddhism also coexists with elements of older indigenous traditions in every country. The villagers call on various gods and spirits for help with harvests, possession, and sickness. Monks may be invited to offer their blessings as part of family rituals for births, marriages, and deaths, even though the ceremonies themselves are not performed by the Buddhist clergy. Monks chant to bring rain, bless the harvest, and pray for the sick. In these popular traditions, the monks can bring merit and blessings to the people, but the Theravada Buddhist tradition itself has little relevance to community ceremonies or life rituals because it was designed primarily as a monastic path to liberation, not a communal religion.

To some extent, the sharp division between monastic and lay practices was blurred in the nineteenth and twentieth centuries. In Sri Lanka, reaction against Christian missionaries and foreign rule, combined with urbanization and the appearance of a middle class, contributed to the rise of what has been called "Protestant Buddhism." This movement was influenced by the Theosophists, especially Henry Olcott, who, as we have noted, helped establish Buddhist schools as an alternative to Western schools with Christian curricula. In this modernized Buddhism, the popular practices were seen as Hindu borrowings and corruptions, whereas the monastic practices were promoted as the true Buddhist teachings and prescribed for everyone. Thus, even layfolk were told they should meditate and expect to be able to attain *nirvana*. Protestant Buddhism also emphasized the rational, scientific nature of the Buddha's teachings, which made them compatible with Western science and modern life. These modifications have had more effect on the small urban populations than on the more traditional rural populations.

In Thailand, the compatibility of Buddhism and modern science played a part in the state-supported modernization process set in motion at the end of the nineteenth century. The religion was spiritualized and de-mythologized. Heaven and hell became states of mind and pedagogical devices instead of actual places. The universe was depicted as essentially moral, and Buddhism was promoted as a system for spiritual and ethical welfare. The presence of saintly monks, who have attained high states of meditation, has operated to keep a balance between this new emphasis on rationalism and morality and the old monastic effort to live a spiritual life culminating in enlightenment.

Theravada in California

California probably has the largest number of Buddhists in the United States, mostly because of its long history of contact with China and Japan. Immigrants from East Asia have established temples in California, and in the 1960s, Japanese Buddhism in particular began to gain popularity among Westerners interested in Eastern religion. The Buddhist emphasis on attainment through an internalized path based on self-effort, with clearly described meditation techniques and no reliance on a savior deity, was well suited to an era of dissatisfaction with traditional Christianity. Because of the contact with East Asia, most of the Buddhist groups in the United States were based on Mahayana traditions. Only after wars in Asia spurred an influx of refugees and the 1965 changes in immigration law granted access to Asians seeking economic opportunities in America did Theravada Buddhism take hold in the United States.

During the first part of the twentieth century, Theravada Buddhism in the United States was limited to a few scholars teaching at colleges. A group of Sri Lankan monks had taken part in the Parliament of Religions in Chicago in 1893, but interest in the Theravada tradition was mostly the province of Western intellectuals who studied the Pali Canon. In 1964, the Most Venerable Madihe Pannaseeha, a Sri Lankan monk, visited the United States and noted the growing interest in Buddhism. In response, the Sasana Sevaka Society of Maharagama, Sri Lanka, sent the Venerable Thera Bope Vinita to Washington, D.C., in 1965. There he founded the Washington Vihara Society, with assistance from the Sri Lankan embassy. The center is run by Sri Lankan monks, but it also receives support from the government of Thailand. Government officials from all over Southeast Asia who are stationed in Washington use it. Since 1965, immigrants from Sri Lanka, Burma, Cambodia, and Thailand have been settling on both coasts of the United States, and their numbers grew rapidly during the 1970s and 1980s. Some of these immigrants, especially those from Southeast Asia, were refugees and came from a wide range of social classes. They have begun to organize centers and even temples for Buddhist practices, sometimes in mixed cultural groups, but more often dividing along national-linguistic lines.

Sri Lankans established several centers in California, such as the California Buddhist Vihara in Concord in 1977, the Los Angeles Buddhist Vihara in Hollywood in 1978, and the Dharma Vijaya Buddhist Vihara in 1980. Most of the immigrants from Sri Lanka are members of an urbanized middle class who speak fluent English, a legacy of the British occupation. Perhaps because of this middle-class dominance, the laicization that characterizes Protestant Buddhism in Asia is evident in the Sri Lankan Theravada groups being established in the United States. Layfolk are being encouraged to spend time on the traditional monastic practices of meditation and study by taking part in retreats and study classes led by monks.

A similar emphasis on providing scripture study classes and meditation retreats is evident in the California Burmese and Thai communities, even though the Burmese and Thai immigrants are not predominantly from middle-class backgrounds. Most of the Southeast Asians came to the United States as refugees fleeing the wars that have spred across their homelands in the last few decades. Consequently, they come from all levels of society, with diverse educational backgrounds and skills. The highly educated have found employment in American society, although seldom in the fields for which they were originally trained. Many of the uneducated agriculturalists have ended up in ethnic ghettos with little hope of achieving economic success. These densely populated communities allow immigrants to interact almost exclusively with members of their own culture and slow the process of assimilation for the first generation.

Possibly because these immigrants came to the United States out of necessity rather than a desire to become Americans, many of them express a desire to return to their homelands when and if conditions improve. The hope for peace and a chance to return to Asia undoubtedly fuels efforts to preserve cultural traditions by organizing religious societies. Burmese immigrants founded the Theravada Buddhist Society of America, Daly City, in 1979, and the Taungpulu Kaba-Aye Monastery in Boulder Creek in 1981. Thai immigrants have gone out of their way to make their centers available for the international community. The Wat Thai in North Hollywood was established with the expressed purpose of including members of all the Theravada groups in Southern California, and the Wat Buddha Godan in Highland is an international meditation center with Vietnamese, Cambodian, and Laotian members. These and other centers remain closely connected to the monasteries in Asia, which send traveling monks to teach in the West.

The largest Theravada temple in the United States is the Wat Thai in North Hollywood. This temple ministers to the largest Thai community outside of Thailand. There are usually about twenty monks in residence, who follow traditional monastic life as well as possible in a different culture. Some of these monks have devoted their entire lives to Buddhism; others are Thais who have taken monastic vows temporarily, in order to improve their spiritual lives, and will remain for only a few months. The monks eat only two meals a day, breakfast and lunch, as prescribed by the Buddha. They have chanting and meditation practices in the morning and evening and spend their afternoons doing work such as counselling, preaching, and printing Buddhist materials. There are occasions when urban American life demands a breach of tradition, such as a monk driving himself to the grocery store if there is no layperson available, but the lifestyle is kept as traditional as possible.

The monks serve the daily needs of their cultural community as well as follow their own life of discipline. They hold small merit-making ceremonies throughout the year on special days such as birthdays, weddings, and memorial and funeral occasions. There are a number of annual festivals in which the whole community gathers to celebrate Buddhist holy days and Thai holidays. Wat Thai also offers activities and services to bring Thai culture to American-born Thai children as well as to the Thai adults. These classes are usually open to anyone who is interested in Thai culture. There are Buddhist Sunday school classes and summer courses teaching Thai language and culture specifically designed for Thai-American children. Summer novice ordination ceremonies are held for youths between the ages of ten and fifteen to introduce them to a greater understanding of Buddhism and Thai culture. Thai classical dance and Thai vegetable carving classes are open to adults, and Thai language classes are available for non-Thais. Wat Thai provides meeting space for clubs and associations as well as religious gatherings. It is very much the cultural center of the Southern California Thai community.

The Cambodian immigrants, who form the second large Theravada community in Southern California, have not been in the United States as long as the Thais and consequently have not set up any religious institutions as large as Wat Thai, only smaller centers. The largest concentration of Cambodians in America is in Long Beach. This community traces its roots back to a student exchange program that brought Cambodians over to study at the California State University in Long Beach. These students returned home, but when war threw their homeland into chaos, they came back to the United States as refugees and settled in the area they already knew from their previous sojourn in America. These refugees then reached out to help their compatriots, and the community grew. Cambodians who are settled in other parts of the United States by the government soon hear about Long Beach and migrate to California to live in "Pnom Penh by the Sea."

The first wave of Cambodian refugees came from the educated elite and made a fairly smooth transition to American society. They had to struggle to learn a new language and find jobs, but today most of them are employed, often in their own businesses. The second wave of refugees was made up of rural farmers who had never had an opportunity or need for education. They have found the adjustment to American life terribly difficult and have largely become a welfare community, dependent on the state. Unlike the Indians and Sri Lankans who have moved into the middle class because of their English literacy and advanced educations, they live in crowded, ethnic enclaves in housing conditions that are well below American standards (but a great improvement over conditions in Cambodia). Yet despite the general poverty of the immigrant community, they still pool their resources to support a few Buddhist monks.

The importance of Buddhism to the Theravada communities from all these countries is evident in their commitment to establish centers in America and maintain monks, who, as in Asia, are dependent on the laity for their livelihood. The community pays for the upkeep of the monks and the residential center where the monks live and teach. The monks generally prefer not to beg in the traditional fashion in order to avoid problems with Westerners, so food offerings are brought to them by the laity. The monks instruct people in Buddhist teachings and practices, and take part in traditional ceremonies by offering blessings and providing the community with the opportunity to earn merit through support of the clergy. Traditional ordination services are now available for Asian-Americans who wish to join the Sangha in California.

Ideally, Theravada Buddhist centers have several buildings to fill a range of functions. There is usually a central sacred building which serves as a temple, a hall for monastic study and public meetings, a *stupa* containing sacred relics, small buildings which serve as residences for monks and guests, and an open area where special activities such as festivals may take place. In California, many of the centers which began with just enough space to house one or two monks now have facilities for all these functions. Some centers offer regular services, held on Sundays in an adaptation to American life, or on full-moon days. These services may include a sermon on the Buddha's teachings, group discussion of the teachings, and a recitation of the Ten Precepts which govern Buddhist life. Some centers offer Sunday school classes specifically designed for children. Special celebrations include Wesak, the spring celebration of the Buddha, and, for Sri Lankans, Olcott Day, celebrated to honor Henry Olcott's efforts to preserve their tradition. Most centers also have facilities for meditation retreats. The retreats allow people to temporarily live a monastic life, for a weekend, ten days, or even three months. The shorter retreats are something of a concession to the exigencies of American life, but the practice of taking vows for a short period of time and devoting oneself to a course of study and meditation in the monastery before returning to ordinary life is a long-standing Theravada tradition, which has come to be widely practiced in recent years as a result of the rise of Protestant Buddhism.

The majority of the people using the Theravada Buddhist facilities are Sri Lankans and Southeast Asians, but the number of non-Asians is also growing. Buddhism is a missionary religion, and part of the impetus for the establishment of Theravada centers in the United States is the desire to improve the understanding of the Buddha's teachings among Westerners. The Buddhists are open to potential converts from Western countries, and there has been a strong outreach program working to make books on Buddhism available in English. The Sri Lankan monks, who have the advantage of speaking English, offer classes on Buddhism that are readily accessible to the American English-speaking community. Westerners are particularly interested in meditation since, unlike traditional Theravadins, they do not consider meditation something that should be reserved for monks. Thus, Euro-Americans often form the majority of the people taking part in weekly meditation programs or using retreat facilities.

Although most of the Theravada centers offer classes in Pali and the vernacular language of their monastic community (Sinhalese, Burmese, Thai), the Buddhists are quite willing to use English in services as they adapt their tradition to its new setting. The Buddha himself told his followers to teach in the vernacular languages. This makes it much easier for the Buddhists to share the Dhamma with Americans and will also help prevent the formation of a linguistic barrier between first- and second-generation Asian-Americans, which has been so problematic in other transplanted religions. The second generation, which has grown up in California, does not share the first generation's longing to return to the old country.

These American children have no memories of a pre-communist Asia and no desire to exchange their current situation for agricultural life. Although most of the second generation consider Buddhism part of their cultural heritage, they really only follow Buddhist practices during festivals. The old tradition of spending a few months or a year in a monastery, establishing a foundation of Buddhist scholarship and meditative practices for one's lifestyle before taking on the burdens of earning a living and starting a family, has not been part of life in modern California. Thus, for the second generation, Theravada Buddhism is, in general, becoming a part of cultural identity, but the personal practices of meditation and study of the Dhamma are once again being relegated to ordained monks rather than making up part of the education of the individual.

Tibetan Buddhism

Buddhism first entered Tibet from India and China in the seventh century, but the eighth-century Indian teacher Padmasambhava is traditionally credited with establishing the Dhamma in the mountain regions north of India. Padmasambhava founded the first monastery, Samye, in Lhasa in 749. Buddhism received early royal support, possibly because the Tibetan king was expanding his reign and sought to unify the areas he conquered by promoting Buddhism as one religion for all the people in place of the diverse local traditions. During the subsequent period of political instability Buddhism declined, but it was revived in the eleventh century. Teachers were invited to Tibet from India to found new monasteries and organize new translations of Indian texts. In the following century, Buddhism spread rapidly. When the Mongols invaded Tibet in the thirteenth century, the monasteries were the major social organizations in the area. Consequently, political responsibility for Tibet was conferred on the leader of the Sakya sect. Later this rulership shifted to the Gelugpa sect. The head of the Gelugpas was known as the Dalai Lama. He became both the religious and temporal ruler of Tibet in the seventeenth century. In the eighteenth century, when Tibet was under the dominion of the Manchu rulers of China, Buddhism continued to be a powerful force and spread even further into northen Asia. In 1959, when the Chinese communists entered Tibet, many of the religious teachers, who were also civil leaders, fled the country. Some settled in India or Bhutan. Over time, many have come to England and the United States.

Tibetan Buddhist schools may be divided into three groups.

They differ over which texts they hold authoritative, which deities receive the most attention, and sometimes over which practices they emphasize, but they share the same general features. The first school is that of the Nyingma, the "old ones," who represent the first wave of Buddhism. Nyingma began as the normal everyday Buddhism of Tibet and only became organized into a coherent school with a canon of accepted texts in reaction to later "reform" movements. The second group, which stemmed from the eleventh-century spread of Buddhism, is represented by the Kargyupa and Sakyapa sects. These schools, describing themselves as reformers of the older tradition, place greater emphasis on monastic discipline. Finally, in the fifteenth century, the Gelugpas, or Yellow Hats, emerged as a third school. The Gelugpas placed great emphasis on monastic discipline and learning, and postponed advanced meditation practices until the end of a long course of study. As mentioned above, the Dalai Lama is the leader of the Gelugpas.

The Tibetan Buddhist tradition drew on both Chinese and Indian sources, but the main emphasis came from the northern areas of India. The Tibetans are thus the heirs to the Vajrayana tradition which grew out of Mahayana Buddhism. Like all other Buddhists, they study the Tipitaka and follow the basic doctrines taught by the Buddha. They emphasize the path of the *bodhisattva*, believing that individuals may attain the highest knowledge and then out of compassion share that knowledge with others. However, whereas in most Mahayana sects the path takes many lifetimes, Vajrayana practices are supposed to make it possible for one to attain enlightenment in the present lifetime.

The core practices of this fast track include repetition of *mantra*s (sacred utterances), performance of *mudra*s (particular gestures), and *sadhana*s (visualizations). These practices require the guidance of a teacher, a *lama*, who already possesses the final knowledge. The *lama* tailors his instructions to the needs of the individual. These instructions will determine what *mantra* one uses and what one visualizes. The *lama* is so important to the Tibetan tradition that sometimes taking "refuge in the teacher" is included as the fourth refuge. *Lama*s are not always monastics in Tibet. Especially among the Nyingma tradition, it is quite possible for *lama*s to marry and have a regular family life, and even those sects that insist on a stricter monastic life acknowledge the credentials of their married brethren.

Some *lama*s, called *tulku*s, are believed to be reincarnations of deceased teachers. A *lama* may leave clues before his death about where he will reappear, and if the clues are not very good, it may take years and the aid of oracles and visions to locate the reincarnation. The child's incarnate status will often be revealed by miracles that accompany his birth, such as a tree blooming in the middle of winter, by his innate serenity and wisdom, or by his ability to identify objects that belonged to the deceased *lama*. The idea of the teacher who returns to his people is linked to the ideal of the *bodhisattva*, the potential Buddha who delays *nirvana* to aid others. The Dalai Lama is believed to be an incarnation of Avalokiteshvara, the *bodhisattva* of compassion.

The name Vajrayana means "diamond path." The diamond referred to is the eternal Buddha-nature resident in all beings. The spiritual exercises known as tantric practices were designed to help the seeker realize his identification with this inner Buddha-nature. These practices involve traditional methods of *yoga* and meditation supplemented with visualizations and the utterance of *mantra*s. The visualizations are based on an elaborate concept about the presence of the Buddha in the world. According to Tibetan tradition, there are five Jinas, "conquerors," also known as heavenly Buddhas—Vairocana (illuminator), Akshobya (imperturbable), Ratnasambhava (jewel-born), Amitabha (boundless light), and Amoghasiddhi (infallible success). These each embody one aspect of divine wisdom, and together they constitute the body of the universe. In a series of equations, the five Jinas are identified with the five aggregates of the individual, the five directions of the cosmos (center, east, west, north, south), the five kinds of evil, and the five kinds of wisdom. In meditation, one visualizes oneself taking the form of a particular Buddha-figure. To do so, one must have a clear image of the Buddhas and their appropriate contexts, with attendant *bodhisattva*s and deities. This practice of visualization fostered the ornate Tibetan paintings of Buddhas surrounded by various sages, demons, and *bodhisattva*s, often residing in different realms. These paintings, called *mandalas*, serve in turn as meditation aids. The process of visualization accompanied by repetition of certain *mantra*s should be carried out in accord with the instructions of a qualified teacher. Other practices include ritual services such as making offerings to deities.

Tibetans in California

Unlike the other Asian traditions discussed in this book, Tibetan Buddhist monks did not come to California to meet the needs of communities of Tibetan immigrants. The Tibetan religious teachers in California were refugees who fled from Chinese communism in

1959 and set out to find new places where they could preserve and pass on their teachings. Some Tibetan teachers believe that their presence in America is fulfilling a prophecy made by Padmasambhava, the founder of the Nyingma sect, who said, "When the iron bird flies, and horses run on wheels,/ The Tibetan people will be scattered like ants across the world,/ And the Dharma will come to the land of the Red Man." The Tibetans have come west for the expressed purpose of sharing their Dharma with Americans.

The first teacher to reach California was Tarthang Tulku. As a child, he was recognized as an incarnate *lama* and his childhood was spent in religious training. When he was fourteen, he began a thirteen-year period of intensive meditation and study under *lama*s representing all the sects of Tibetan Buddhism. He was the abbot of a large Nyingmapa monastery when the Chinese entered Tibet. In 1959, he fled to Sikkim, a state in northeastern India. A gifted scholar, proficient in Tibetan, Sanskrit, Pali, Hindi, and English, he was then sent by the Dalai Lama to teach in Benares, India.

Tarthang Tulku arrived in Berkeley in 1969, and the small group that quickly formed around him became the nucleus of the Tibetan Nyingma Meditation Center. Tarthang Tulku saw Americans as sincere seekers with an interest in truth and spiritual life. He taught them a very traditional form of Vajrayana practice, but made a point of carefully preparing his students for these practices, which came from a completely different culture. He was also quite willing to use American concepts of science and psychology to explain teachings in ways that would make sense to his Western audience. Traditionally, disciples of the Nyingma tradition were members of a community of family groups centered around a *lama*, who, more often than not, was married. The practices had long been adapted to the needs of householders and did not require Americans to live a monastic life.

American students under Tulku began where a Tibetan would begin, with the first of the tantric preliminary practices, which consists of a hundred thousand prostrations. The entire body must be prostrated on the ground while the student recites the threefold refuge and visualizes *buddha*s, *bodhisattva*s, *lama*s, and saints of the Nyingma lineage. This is not only hard physical work, but it demands openness and surrender, the setting aside of resistance. After the prostrations, which may take weeks, months, or even years, there follow the other four "hundred thousand" preliminary practices: a hundred thousand repetitions of the *bodhisattva* vow, a hundred thousand repetitions of the Vajrasattva *mantra*, a hundred thousand offerings of a *mandala* representing the entire universe, and a hundred thousand repetitions of Padmasambhava's *mantra*. All of these were to be accompanied by specific visualizations. Students were also given instruction in meditation, starting with training in proper posture.

As the group grew, they moved into larger quarters, and more settled patterns of practice evolved. There was an hour of prostration and sitting every morning, walking meditation, chanting, and prostrations in the evening. Rituals, such as *pujas* and *sutra* readings, were held regularly. Moreover, since the chanting was in Tibetan, students began to study the language. Tarthang Tulku worked closely with his small band of followers, training them in traditional fashion, with the expectation that they would become the future teachers of Nyingma in America.

Tarthang Tulku also established the Nyingma Institute in 1973 as a secular school to accommodate the mental health professionals, academics, and members of the general public who wanted to learn about the Tibetan tradition. Study at the Institute combined instruction in the psychological, philosophical, and experiential insights of the Nyingma lineage through a mixture of teaching and meditation. In addition, the Nyingma Center owns the Dharma Publishing House and puts out books on Tibetan Buddhism as well as an annual journal. They have also built a large retreat center in Sonoma County, called Odiyan, where Tibetan culture is being preserved in a cultural center and Tibetan knowledge is being applied in the use of traditional architecture.

Other teachers have founded Nyingmapa centers in California. The Chapori-Ling Foundation Sangha in San Franciso, for example, was established by Dr. Norbu L. Chen from Nepal. He was trained by Tibetan refugees who settled in Nepal after 1959. The Foundation operates a college which offers courses for prospective monks and nuns and specializes in traditional medicinal practices. Yeshe Nyingpo, a Nyingma organization founded in New York by His Holiness Dujom Rinpoche, has a center in Berkeley. This organization has taken on the mission of spreading the Dhamma in the West and describes itself as the instrument for the transmission of the pure Nyingmapa teachings and practice.

The second branch of Tibetan Buddhism to be established in California is associated with Chogyam Trungpa (1939–1987), the founder of the Naropa Institute in Colorado. Chogyam Trungpa was the tenth incarnation of the *lama* Trungpa Tulku. As such, he was educated in a Kargyupa monastery. After his escape from Tibet during the communist takeover, Chogyam Trungpa attended Oxford University and then went to Scotland, where he established the Samye-Ling Meditation Center. During his years in Scotland, Chogyam Trungpa became convinced that he could teach in the West more effectively as a layman than as a monk. After careful reflection, he discarded his robes, saying it was necessary "to do away with the 'exotic' externals which were too fascinating to students in the West." Shortly thereafter, he married a young English woman and moved to the United States.

An emphasis on meditation and a rejection of external formalities marked Chogyam Trungpa's teachings from this point on. At the Tail of the Tiger community in Vermont, the Karma Dzong Meditation Center in Boulder, and at the many small centers in California, Chogyam Trungpa focused on teaching the practices of Tibetan Buddhism. He did not try to regulate his students' lifestyles, yet many of the young people who came to join the communities in the early days from the hippie counterculture stopped using drugs after practicing meditation for a few weeks. Chogyam Trungpa was not concerned with how people dressed, what they ate, or whether or not they used drugs; his major concern was teaching Tibetan Buddhism. In the matter of spiritual practices, he actively guided his students. He suggested various techniques to meet individual needs and had most students practice fairly simple meditations, with little use of the *mantras* and *mudras* that characterize Tibetan practices. More advanced students moved on to more sophisticated traditional Tibetan meditation techniques, but their progress was slow. Tibetan teachers such as Trungpa have been very aware that their American students are coming out of a cultural background in which Buddhism has not been part of their lives, so they are not yet prepared for many of the traditional practices. As one teacher put it, "They can't start at the Ph.D. level when they are just ready for kindergarten."

Chogyam Trungpa wanted to teach Americans to develop a "Buddhist outlook." He felt that when Americans became dissatisfied with the basic teachings of Christianity and then became fascinated with the colorful robes and rituals of Asian religions, they were getting caught up in externals, which really meant that they were still involved in materialism. He advocated the development of American lay Buddhism rather than monasticism, saying that through meditation one cuts through the fascination with externals and penetrates to the heart of matters. Chogyam Trungpa thought Buddhism was ideal for the Western mind because it is scientific and practical. But he saw it as a spiritual practice that would influence art, music, and psychology, not as an institutionalized "church."

Despite the early death of Chogyam Trungpa, his peculiar form of Tibetan Buddhism remains strong to this day. At the San Francisco Dharmadhatu center, for example, people regularly meet for programs several times a week. Some programs include an hour of meditation followed by a tape of one of Chogyam Trungpa's talks and a discussion of the tape. On weekends there are day-long meditations, broken by meals and work periods. Meditation sessions include recitation of the Threefold Refuge and chanting.

There is also an independent Kargyupa center (not related to Karma Dzong) in San Francisco. The Kagya Droden Choling was founded by Kalu Rinpoche, who has trained a number of monks especially to head centers in the West. He has a center in Darjeeling, India, and during the 1970s he started centers in Europe and North America. Each center follows a regular format of worship and meditation. The Kagya Droden Choling also publishes books in Tibetan and English.

Ewam Choden in Kensington, California, was the first center for the Sakyapa sect in the United States. Ewam Choden means "the integration of method and wisdom, compassion and emptiness, and possessing the Dharma (the true way of life taught by the Buddha)." It was founded in 1971 by Lama Kunga Thartse Rinpoche. The head of the sect, Sakya Trizin, paid his first visit to the center in 1977. The center was designed to encourage practice and study of Tibetan culture as well as religion. There is a program of meditation, classes, and observation of traditional holy days. The center also administers a Tibetan Relief Fund.

The Thubten Dhargye Ling Tibetan Center for Buddhist Studies in Los Angeles was founded in 1979 by Geshe Tsultrim Gyeltsen, a teacher in the Gelugpa tradition. The center's name, which means "Land of Increasing Buddha's Teachings," was given by the Dalai Lama. The Dalai Lama sent Geshe Gyeltsen to England as the director of Tibet House in the 1960s, and in 1976 Geshe Gyeltsen came to the United States, where he taught at the University of California, Santa Barbara, and the University of Oriental Studies in Los Angeles. He has continued his close relationship with the Dalai Lama, hosting his visits to Los Angeles. The center has weekly services on Sunday mornings, special monthly ceremonies, meditation courses, and weekend seminars.

The Vajrapani Institute for Wisdom Culture in Boulder Creek,

California, is also part of the Gelugpa Order. It was established by Lama Thubten Yeshe and Lama Thubten Zopa Rinpoche. Both refugees from Tibet, they met in 1959 when they settled in Buxaduar, India. The young Zopa Rinpoche was sent to Thubten Yeshe for further instruction in Buddhism. Along with a Buddhist nun, the two monks established the Nepal Mahayana Gompa Center near Kathmandu in 1969. The Nepalese center soon began to attract Western students, and, in 1973, an organization of Western monks and nuns called the International Mahayana Institute was founded. In 1974, the two monks were invited to tour the West by C.T. Shen of the Institute for Advanced Study of World Religions in New York. While in America, they established the Bodhicitta Center for Developing Human Potential in Indiana. The publication and circulation of the lectures given during this tour brought them more students and the eventual development of other centers. In 1977, students donated thirty acres of land near Boulder Creek, California, for the establishment of a retreat center called Vajrapani Institute, which became the American headquarters of the movement.

The *lama*s establishing centers in the United States are consciously spreading their Dhamma to a new land. In the process, there is some disagreement among the *lama*s about how much Tibetan culture they need to teach their new students in order to provide the correct context for the religious practices. All seem to agree, however, that if the basic teachings of the Vajrayana path are not to be diluted, then American students will require a lengthy period of preparation before they can take on the more advanced meditation techniques. This, it should be emphasized, is not because the *lama*s believe Westerners are somehow less "spiritual" than Tibetans; it is because Westerners are not raised in the traditional cultural milieu. The Tibetans assume that their American students will study and practice in the traditional way until they can become the next generation of teachers, and that they will then preserve this tradition, which has been lost, for the most part, in its homeland amid the Himalayas. This transplanting of Tibetan Buddhism seems to be successful; in 1988 for the first time, a *tulku* (reincarnated *lama*) was born on the east coast of the United States.

Bibliography

Bunnag, Jane. *Buddhist Monk, Buddhist Layman.* London: Cambridge University Press, 1973.

Carrithers, Michael. *The Forest Monks of Sri Lanka.* Delhi: Oxford University Press, 1983.

Ellwood, Robert S. and Partin, Harry B. *Religious and Spiritual Groups in Modern America.* New Jersey: Prentice Hall, 1988.

Fields, Rick. *How the Swans Came to the Lake: A Narrative History of Buddhism in America.* Boulder: Shambala, 1981.

Gombrich, Richard. *Theravada Buddhism.* London and New York: Routledge, 1988.

Layman, Emma McCloy. *Buddhism in America.* Chicago: Nelson Hall, 1976.

Melton, Gordon, editor. *The Encyclopedia of American Religions,* Third Edition. Detroit: Gale Research Inc., 1989.

Morreale, Don, editor. *Buddhist America.* Santa Fe: John Muir Publications, 1988.

Ong, Paul; Bonacich, Edna; and Cheng, Lucie, editors. *The New Asian Immigration in Los Angeles and Global Restructuring.* Philadelphia: Temple University Press, 1994.

Richardson, E. Allen. *East Comes West: Asian Religions and Cultures in North America.* New York: The Pilgrim Press, 1985.

Robinson, Richard H. and Johnson, Willard L. *The Buddhist Religion.* Belmont: Wadsworth Publishing Co., 1982.

Shaw, Scott. *Cambodian Refugees in Long Beach, California: The Definitive Study.* Hermosa Beach: Buddha Rose Publications, 1989.

Snellgrove, David. *Indo-Tibetan Buddhism.* Boston: Shambala Publications, Inc., 1987.

Tamney, Joseph B. *American Society in the Buddhist Mirror.* New York and London: Garland Publishing, Inc., 1992.

5 American Approaches to South Asian Spirituality

Although South Asian religions did not have a profound impact on nor generate large mass movements amongst Americans of European descent until the 1960s, South Asian religious thought nevertheless has had a long and venerable history in America. This chapter will explore the history of South Asian religious ideas in America since the end of the eighteenth century, following their path to California. To do so, we will examine in detail three American religious movements that were founded in response to South Asian religious ideas in the nineteenth century: Transcendentalism, Theosophy, and Vedanta. Although small in scale when compared to some of the other American religious movements spawned in that century, these three traditions were to have a significant impact on the United States at large, and, in the case of Theosophy and Vedanta, on California in particular.

Early American approaches to South Asian spirituality find their origins in the tangled skein of attitudes generated by two intellectual movements which swept Europe and America during the eighteenth and early nineteenth centuries. These movements are now known as rationalism and romanticism. Europe and America spent much of the mid-eighteenth century in the thrall of rationalism. Rationalists took their metaphors and approach to the world from the natural sciences, which, starting with Newton, had begun to yield spectacular results in the early part of that century. Indeed, it was felt by many of the thinkers of this "Age of Enlightenment" that all the problems of humanity—including cultural problems—could be understood and solved by an application of the scientific method of objective observation, hypothesis, and experiment. Such attitudes opened all facets of European society to scrutiny, including

Christianity, the reigning religion of Europe. For the first time in centuries, the hegemonic grip of Christianity was weakened somewhat in the West.

Thus one of the legacies of rationalism in the West was an underlying cultural relativism. Treating Christianity as an object of investigation and not as an object of faith led to the observation that Christianity had many things in common with other religions of the world. There arose the idea that religion was something more fundamental than Christianity, and that while Christianity might be religion's highest expression, perhaps all religions shared the same rudimentary elements. One way of getting at this problem was to investigate the elements that went into religions of other peoples. For many Europeans, India was the place to look if one wanted to investigate the full range of religious experience and possibilities. The entrenchment of the British *raj* in the eighteenth century had paved the way for increased access to and exposure of Indian ideas and traditions. Scholars, both European and Indian, began to translate and publish the ancient Sanskrit texts in English, and these texts found eager readers on both sides of the Atlantic. Benjamin Franklin, for example, was a good friend and admirer of the English Sanskritist Sir William Jones; and among the Unitarians of New England, the translations of Indian religious texts by the Hindu reformer Ram Mohan Roy (1774–1833) were especially favored.

The skepticism inherent in rationalism eventually created a backlash in favor of faith and the quest for transcendental experience. In time, this backlash coalesced into an intellectual countermovement known today as romanticism. Some romantics attempted to revive Christianity, either by stressing its emotional appeal or by constructing philosophical proofs of its reasonableness. A few others, however, hopelessly dissatisfied with Christianity but still seeking the transcendent element in their lives, fashioned new religious traditions, in part by using the religious resources now coming from abroad. In America, the most successful early attempt in this direction was Transcendentalism.

Transcendentalism and South Asian Thought

Transcendentalism was a religious system built on the belief that nature and the human soul share a common structure, an idea one modern historian of religions has called the "doctrine of correspondences." By contemplating nature, the transcendentalists argued, one could make an intuitive connection between one's mind and the structure of the universe—a connection through which the wisdom of the cosmos would flow and the presence of God could be felt. For Transcendentalists, both God and revelation were inherent in the human soul.

Although Transcendentalism could never boast of an institutional structure, it did have a leader: Ralph Waldo Emerson (1803–1882), a Unitarian clergyman turned freelance philosopher, whose 1832 book, *Nature*, defined the Transcendental movement. Emerson's Transcendentalism was an eclectic philosophy and took material from any source which corroborated its central tenets. At first, Emerson was uninterested in South Asian thought; indeed, during his boyhood, Emerson's aunt, herself a staunch Unitarian, had tried to introduce him to the translations of Ram Mohan Roy, but without much success. Emerson's appreciation for South Asian thought grew, however, as his Unitarianism evolved into Transcendentalism. While still taking most of his vocabulary from continental philosophers (such as Kant), Emerson nevertheless became increasingly taken by the correspondences between Indian thought and his own. Many of the translations of the Asiatic Society of Bengal—texts such as the *Laws of Manu*, *Ramayana*, *Bhagavadgita*, *Mahabharata*, the Puranas, the *Rig Veda*—made their way to Emerson's Concord, Massachusetts, study.

Transcendentalism as Emerson conceived it was first and foremost a species of pantheism. God is everywhere, Emerson argued, and can be discerned in anything: "What is there divine in a load of bricks? What is there divine in a barber's shop? Much. All." And against the cosmic separation between man and God inherent in the indigenous Calvinism of New England, man *was* God in Emerson's thought. In his famous "Divinity School Address" and in numerous other essays, Emerson taught that since God is the substratum of all souls, every soul could therefore know transcendence, every soul could become divine. Emerson was thus attracted to the monism of ancient Indian thought. Indeed, the relationship between man and Emerson's God—the "Over-Soul" as he called it—struck the philosopher as analogous to the *atman* and its relationship to Brahman in classical Hinduism. As in the illustration of the salt mixed with water, which appears in the *Chandogya Upanishad*, the Hindu Brahman and Emerson's Over-Soul are inseparable from the world. And just as the dissolved salt gives the tang to the characterless water, so, too, did Brahman and the Over-Soul give the spark to each individual soul. "Within man is the soul of the whole," Emerson wrote, "the universal beauty, to which every part and particle is equally related; the eternal One."

There were, of course, profound differences between Emerson's thought and ancient Indian thought. Emerson's God, even with its impersonal title of "Over-Soul," always remained an essentially personal God. And Emerson could never quite bring himself to abandon completely the notion of individual personality. However, he did accept two other important doctrines from classical Hinduism: *maya* and *karma*. In terms of *maya*, Emerson wrote in his *Journal* that

> In the history of intellect [there is] no more important fact than the Hindu theology, teaching [as it does] that the beatitude or supreme good is to be attained through science: namely, by the perception of the real and the unreal, setting aside matter, and qualities and affections or emotions and persons, and actions, as Mayas or illusions, and thus arriving at the contemplation of the one eternal Life and Cause, and a perpetual approach and assimilation to Him. . . .

Emerson accepted the idea of *maya* as the *modus operandi* of the universe, a tool by which the individual soul was brought to knowledge: "Youth, age, property, condition, events, persons, self, are only successive *maya*s, through which Vishnu mocks and instructs the soul." Emerson devoted one of his more successful essays, entitled "Illusion," to the concept of *maya*.

The doctrine of *karma* was also central to Emerson's later transcendental system. Almost instinctively rejecting the twin Calvinist ideas of election and predestination in youth, and abetted by an early reading of the Upanishads and the *Bhagavadgita*, Emerson early on was confirmed in his belief in *karma*, and extolled it in his essay "Compensation." Only with the idea of reincarnation was Emerson uneasy: his restless progressivism made the long rollercoaster ride of the Hindu soul unattractive. As a young man at least, he had difficulty accepting the idea that moral evolution was anything but unidirectional. As he grew older, however, and as his certainty of personal immortality waned, he came more and more to entertain in his *Journal* the complete logic of the Vedantic system.

Throughout his life, in his essays and his poetry, Emerson used both ideas and images taken from South Asian thought and South Asian texts. For example, some have seen his enigmatic poem, "Brahma," as an epitome of the *Bhagavadgita*, while others have seen it as an almost direct quotation from the *Katha Upanishad*. In much of his poetry, however, explicit Hindu mythical images abound: the wheel, for example, the stone egg from which the world is hatched, and the cosmic fig tree, its roots reaching up from the earth and embracing the transcendent. If nothing else, the literature of Transcendentalism exposed Americans for the first time to the technical philosophical vocabulary and mythical imagery of South Asian religious thought.

The impact of Transcendentalism in California is difficult to gauge. Since it lacked any institutional base, it had no permanent presence in the Golden State. We do know, however, that some of California's most effective religious leaders in the late nineteenth century, men such as Thomas Starr King, were influenced by Transcendentalism, as were some powerful non-traditional voices such as that of John Muir. How far the specifically South Asian doctrines in Emerson's thought attracted these leaders is, however, impossible to tell. Starr King, for example, was a committed Christian, and no matter how liberal a Protestant environment may have reigned in California, his audiences would not have been ready for the vocabulary of South Asian religion, even if some of its ideas had found their way into his thought. And as for Muir, while it is said that he carried a copy of Emerson's *Nature* in his pocket wherever he went, the naturalist's pronounced anti-dogmatism led him to abandon technical philosophical vocabulary of any kind, thus making it almost impossible to indicate with any precision the sources of his thought. Nevertheless, the fact that Transcendentalist literature was being read in California meant that many were being indirectly exposed to South Asian religious ideas, quite probably for the first time.

Theosophy

The next great wave of interest in South Asian religious thought in America came late in the nineteenth century. This new wave of interest would indeed have a large impact on California, as it resulted in the creation of one of the most durable South Asian-oriented religious traditions to arise in America, Theosophy. Theosophy was initiated by the Russian émigrée, Helena Petrovna Blavatsky (1831–1891), perhaps one of the most interesting characters of the era. After an unsettled youth and an unhappy early marriage, Blavatsky spent a decade wandering the globe before coming to New York in 1873. Blavatsky had an ardent interest in all things esoteric. By the time she came to America, she was especially interested in reviving the Western hermetic and cabalistic tradition.

In 1874, Blavatsky met Colonel Henry Steele Olcott while investigating spirit manifestations in rural Vermont. A lawyer by training and a master administrator by temperament, Olcott was a formidable character in his own right, having distinguished himself in a variety of positions during the Civil War. Shortly after their meeting, Blavatsky and Olcott discovered that they shared similar interests in occult subjects. Together, they decided to found an organization to further investigation into the occult. Dubbed the "Theosophical Society" (from *sophia*, "wisdom," and *theos*, "divine things"), the organization was formally incorporated in New York in 1875. The society had as its primary goal "to collect and diffuse a knowledge of the laws which govern the universe." It was a small group which initially met in a rented hall in Manhattan, and they devoted themselves at first exclusively to book reviews and demonstrations by psychics and mediums. Among its members were a diverse assortment of freethinkers, socialists, feminists, and, perhaps not surprisingly, Transcendentalists. Indeed, in a very real way, the literature of Transcendentalism, replete as it was with the ideas and images of South Asian religion, had paved the way for many an American's interest in and understanding of Theosophy.

During the time of the formation of the Theosophical Society, Madame Blavatsky was hard at work on a monumental two-volume compendium of occult lore which would eventually be called *Isis Unveiled* (1877). Although controversy still surrounds its composition, *Isis Unveiled* remains nevertheless an unparalleled synthesis of occult thought from around the world. It would soon have a major impact on the direction of the infant Theosophical Society. Blavatsky claimed in *Isis Unveiled* that the earth had once known a Golden Age populated by an ancient race distinct from *Homo Sapiens*, whose teachings formed a universal religion which once spanned the globe. This *ur*-religion contained a systematic knowledge of the deepest mysteries of the universe, and its practices allowed every person to tap into his latent psychic powers. This in turn resulted in the flowering of the great ancient civilizations such as Egypt and Greece. As proof of this last claim, Blavatsky pointed to the seemingly obvious similarities between ancient religious symbols and architecture all the way from China to Central America. Moreover—and most tantalizingly—Blavatsky claimed that although this ancient race was now extinct, its "primitive wisdom still survives, and is attainable by those who 'will,' 'dare,' and 'keep silent.'"

Whether or not one accepts the book's syncretic mythology, *Isis Unveiled* is important because it signaled a shift in emphasis in Blavatsky's thought. Instead of recommending the study of exclusively Western esoteric sources, Blavatsky now increasingly pointed to ancient Hindu and Buddhist lore. It is not really known why the shift occurred: Blavatsky herself claimed supernatural influence. Ever since her early wanderings in Asia, Blavatsky had claimed to be in telepathic contact with a strange brotherhood of Tibetan Masters, whom she called either Mahatmas ("Great-Souls") or Adepts. Blavatsky claimed that it was they who had dictated to her large portions of *Isis Unveiled*, and it was they who insisted she turn her attention from the wisdom of the West to the wisdom of the East. It was in the East, the Masters told her, and specifically in India and Ceylon (modern-day Sri Lanka), that the ancient wisdom was to be found still practiced to this day.

Upon the publication of *Isis Unveiled*, Blavatsky and Olcott resolved to travel to India. There they established branches of the Theosophical Society in 1879, first in Bombay, and later in Adyar, near Madras. The move was an important one, since personal contact with South Asian religions allowed them to incorporate many elements of South Asian thought into Theosophical doctrine and thus popularize them in the West.

While in India, Blavatsky and Olcott traveled widely and corresponded with famous Hindu, Buddhist, Parsi, and Jain leaders. Impressed by what they saw and what they heard, they added a new goal to the Theosophical Society's code: "To promote the study of Aryan and other South Asian literature, religions, science, and vindicate its importance." To this end, Blavatsky produced her second great work, *The Secret Doctrine* (1888). Here, Blavatsky incorporated some of the more widespread doctrines of Indian religious thought into her Theosophical system. Reincarnation, which was given little attention in *Isis Unveiled*, now became a keystone in Blavatsky's worldview. So too did *karma* and *nirvana*. Moreover, her belief in the Masters was explicitly associated with the Buddhist idea of the *bodhisattva*, enlightened individuals who either prolong their lives or choose to return to this earth in order to teach others the way. Indeed, Theosophy came to develop quite a pantheon of such *bodhisattva*s, among the most popular of which were Morya and Koot Hoomi, known in Theosophical shorthand as "M." and "K.H."

Theosophy in California

Meanwhile, in the absence of Blavatsky and Olcott, the Theosophical Society in the United States had undergone some major changes. In 1886, William Q. Judge, one of the charter members of the organization, was elected president. Under Judge's energetic leadership, the Theosophical movement in the United States em-

barked on a period of rapid expansion. To aid in its outreach, printing facilities were purchased in 1886 and a society journal began to
appear shortly thereafter. In addition, under the influence of *The
Secret Doctrine*, the American branch of the Theosophical Society
began to produce a series of affordable editions of the *Bhagavadgita*,
the yoga sutras of Pantanjali, and other primary religious texts from
India.

While never a mass movement in the United States, the
Theosophical Society had by the 1890s nevertheless become prominent enough to be an influence on popular culture. In 1891, Judge
wrote that "in the United States [Theosophy] has so often been
heard of, it is a matter of ordinary knowledge; its terms are used in
magazines, its literature widely sold, it has so invaded thought that
novels and stories are constantly written on its lines." By the time
Blavatsky died in 1891, the Theosophical Society had fifty-four
branches in the United States alone and counted among its ranks
hundreds of members. California itself could boast more Theosophist lodges than any other state, and soon events would conspire
to make the Golden State one of the premier centers of Theosophical activities in the entire country.

Upon Helena Blavatsky's death, a power struggle ensued for
control of the Theosophical Society between Olcott in India and
Judge in America. What resulted was a splintering of the Society. In
1895, Judge, with the backing of the majority of American Theosophists, declared the organization separate from the Indian branch,
officially forming the independent Theosophical Society of
America. Of the by-now eighty-nine American branches of Blavatsky's original Theosophical Society, all but fourteen chose to join
this new organization. Upon Judge's death in 1896, the leadership
of the new Theosophical Society of America was temporarily split
between E.T. Hargrove and Katherine Tingley. Tingley, who was an
experienced organizer and successful fund-raiser, was also the pro-
tégée of Judge. A dynamic personality in her own right, Katherine
Tingley's bold vision for the Society's future soon won her the post
of the Society's sole president.

One of Tingley's first acts as president was to unveil her plans to
create a Theosophical community and school in California. This,
she announced, was to be the first step in a world-wide Theosophical crusade to create a global Theosophical Brotherhood. The
California facility needed an endowment, however, so Tingley,
along with five other prominent Theosophists, launched a highly
successful year-long international fund-raising effort. In 1897,

ground was broken for the community at Point Loma, a beautiful headland on the Pacific Coast just north of San Diego.

Katherine Tingley moved forcefully to consolidate her leadership of the Theosophical Society of America. At the Theosophical Convention in Chicago in 1898, she pushed through a new constitution, changed the name of the organization to The Universal Brotherhood and Theosophical Society, and assumed almost dictatorial powers. From then on, Tingley devoted herself almost exclusively to the growth of the Point Loma community. This in itself was no small task. One modern historian of the Point Loma community described the over-three-hundred-acre compound as being like a small city, including "a population of five hundred, three large buildings—two surrounded by aquamarine and amethyst-glass domes which were illuminated at night—groups of smaller bungalows and tents used as dwellings, a Greek theater, forty-foot avenues winding through luxuriant gardens and orchards, and forests of eucalyptus planted on previously unwooded ground."

The primary emphasis at Point Loma was education. Here Tingley established a school for children, a college, and, in 1919, a Theosophical University. Tingley had very distinct theories on the subject of education, especially the education of young children. She believed that only through constant supervision and rigidly imposed structure could the effects of *karma* be somewhat overcome at a social level. Only by creating a child disposed instinctively toward brotherhood and cooperation could mankind as a whole hope to better itself with each incarnation. Tingley called her educational system Raja Yoga, a Sanskrit phrase meaning "Kingly Union." Theosophists from around the country and, indeed, from around the world, sent their offspring there to be educated under Tingley's strict care. In addition to paying students, Tingley also brought a large number of orphans and indigent children from the United States and Cuba to study free of charge at Point Loma. In its heyday, the school could boast more than three hundred students and sixty-five teachers at any one time.

Some Californians were fascinated by the Theosophical work going on at Point Loma, most were indifferent, but some were openly hostile, disapproving of what they called "fanatical cults" in California. Mrs. Tingley, however, was nothing but tenacious in the face of such challenges. When she was personally attacked in print by the *Los Angeles Times* in 1901, she sued the paper for libel and won a $7,500 judgment. When the immigration of Cuban children to Point Loma was halted after an organization called the Society for the Prevention of Cruelty to Children charged that the Point Loma school was a sham, Tingley invited the Commissioner of Immigration to personally inspect the program. The government subsequently allowed the children passage. The most vociferous protest against the community came from local Christian Protestant and Catholic clergy. Four years after the founding of Point Loma, a group of clergymen published a stinging denunciation of Theosophy, calling it both anti-social and anti-Christian. Such tensions continued for years to come.

Point Loma, however, had a more serious, if more mundane, problem: money. The Point Loma colony had survived into the 1920s relying chiefly on contributions from members and tuition charges for the school, which amounted to little. The Wall Street crash of 1928 was therefore a devastating blow. By the time Tingley died the next year, the colony was in serious, and ultimately insurmountable, financial difficulty. Drastic retrenchments were called for, and over the next ten years the colony was gradually liquidated to pay off creditors. By 1940, the community was entirely gone. The successors of Katherine Tingley subsequently scaled back the goals of the organization as a whole, choosing now to focus on publishing and promoting strong local Theosophical organizations. In 1942, the Theosophical Society of America changed its name back to the original Theosophical Society, moving its headquarters first to Los Angeles, and then to Pasadena, where it continues to function under this name.

Krishnamurti

At the same time that Katherine Tingley was consolidating her control over the Theosophical Society of America, an equally powerful and intelligent woman named Annie Besant was consolidating her control over the old Theosophical Society in Adyar, India. This, too, was an event which would eventually have repercussions in California. Annie Besant had met Helena Blavatsky in England in 1888. Impressed by the younger woman, Blavatsky made sure that she rose quickly in the Theosophical ranks. Besant first assumed control as president of the European branch of the Society shortly after the death of Blavatsky, and then, after the death of Olcott in 1907, Besant, now a resident of Adyar, assumed complete control of the original Theosophical Society.

Like Katherine Tingley, Annie Besant had a bold vision for the future of Theosophy, but one that was distinctly different. Near the turn of the century, Mrs. Besant began to talk openly and widely of the inevitable coming of an Avatar, a divine incarnation, who would lead the world into a new stage of evolution. In 1908, during a tour of the United States, she spoke tirelessly of the imminent coming of the World Teacher, a theme she became even more insistent about when she returned to India later that year. Some among the Theosophical Society's membership looked askance at this new doctrine, and the Indian press had a field day ridiculing the idea.

Nevertheless, Besant soon discovered her new World Teacher. It turned out to be a young Indian boy named Jiddu Krishnamurti. Krishnamurti was born in 1895 in a small village in Andhra Pradesh, South India. In 1905, Krishnamurti and his brother were brought to live in Adyar by their father after the death of their mother. Four years later, Krishnamurti and his brother were observed playing on a beach by C.W. Leadbetter, an important Theosophist and confidant of Annie Besant. Once brought to her attention, Besant, too, was immediately taken by Krishnamurti's presence, his silence and natural poise, and agreed with Leadbetter that Krishnamurti would indeed be the earthly vehicle of the new World Teacher. Mrs. Besant quickly gained legal custody of Krishnamurti and embarked him on a strict regimen of intellectual and spiritual training under the watchful eye of Leadbetter. Besant and Krishnamurti soon developed a very close relationship, she addressing him as son, and he addressing her as mother.

From then on, Krishnamurti led an exhaustingly peripatetic life. In 1911, Mrs. Besant traveled with Krishnamurti and his brother to England, where she hoped to prepare the boys for entrance to Oxford. Moreover, she sought to avoid further ridicule for what was called in the Indian press "this Messiah business." Both boys failed to pass the necessary qualifying exams, however, and they were subsequently stranded in England when war broke out in 1914. Nearly a decade passed before Krishnamurti finally returned to his native India in 1921. His stay was a short one, however, for despite the educational debacle in England, Besant still had confidence in Krishnamurti as the new World Teacher, and she soon sent him to be shown off at a major Theosophical convention in Australia organized by C.W. Leadbetter.

Krishnamurti's initial contact with California was nothing less than serendipitous. Due to the illness of Krishnamurti's brother on the trip home, it was decided that the two brothers should postpone their return to Europe and vacation in the reportedly healthful climate of Southern California. The brothers disembarked at San Francisco and traveled south to Los Angeles. Krishnamurti was instantly struck by the beauty of the California countryside, forming an attachment to the state which lasted a lifetime. After touring the Pacific Coast redwoods, which Krishnamurti compared favorably to the cathedrals of Europe, the brothers were invited by A.P. Warrington, the general secretary of the American-Adyar Theosophical Society, to visit Ojai, a small town east of Santa Barbara reputed to be an ancient Native American holy site. There, in the idyllic setting of the rural California countryside, Krishnamurti and his brother settled into a small cottage surrounded by a small orchard.

This was a momentous time and place for Krishnamurti. From August 1922 to November 1923, Krishnamurti underwent a tremendous and painful spiritual experience which he later characterized as the awakening of the *kundalini* energy. This was the first of many spiritual transformations he claimed to have undergone in his lifetime. In honor of Krishnamurti's spiritual awakening there, Annie Besant eventually purchased the Ojai property, naming it *Arya Vihara*, the "Monastery of the Noble Ones."

Meanwhile, Besant remained in India, where she continued to make increasingly inflated claims for Krishnamurti and his status as World Teacher. Annie Besant was also busily pushing through her plans to reorganize the Adyar Theosophical Society on an explicitly religious basis, with Krishnamurti and herself as twin *gurus*. Not surprisingly, this move engendered vigorous dissent among some of the more powerful members of the Society. This dissent, compounded by the facts that Mrs. Besant was also showing signs of age, her behavior was becoming erratic, and her energy flagging, doomed her efforts from the start.

Krishnamurti himself was beginning to have doubts. Although enormously grateful for the time and energy Mrs. Besant had devoted to him and harboring feelings of great filial love, Krishnamurti nevertheless was beginning to rebel. The death of his brother, Nitya, in 1925 had a profound impact on Krishnamurti, and it was from this point on that Krishnamurti began to talk seriously of renouncing his assigned role. Finally, on August 3, 1929, in Ommen, the Netherlands, in the presence of Mrs. Besant, Krishnamurti rejected his messiahship and formally dissolved the Order of the Star, an organization set up by Mrs. Besant to manage the "new age." "This is no magnificent deed," he announced before the group,

> because I do not want any followers. . . . The moment you follow someone you cease to follow Truth. . . . I am concerning myself with only one essential thing: to set man free. I desire to

free him from all cages, from all fears, and not to found religions, new sects, nor to establish new theories and new philosophies. . . . I have only one purpose: to make man free, to urge him towards freedom; to help him break away from all limitations, for that alone will give him eternal happiness, will give him the unconditioned realization of self.

In later years, Krishnamurti was to make the denial of the *guru* a central theme in his thought. The impact of this rejection was nothing short of revolutionary for traditional Hindu thought. For, as one of Krishnamurti's biographers once wrote,

The denial of the *guru* as central to religious inquiry was in India the ultimate negation of all spiritual authority; for in the absence of the one sacred revealed book, the *guru* was the initiator, the preceptor, the doorway to truth. By his refusal to concede the place of any intermediary between the seeker and reality Krishnamurti cast total responsibility on the seeker.

Almost in an Emersonian vein, Krishnamurti exhorted his listeners to look within themselves and within nature for spiritual answers. He told them, too, that while religious ecstasy and extraordinary extrasensory phenomena exist, they are nevertheless not in themselves necessarily a path to truth. Simplicity, clarity of perception, and a continuous examination of one's own consciousness were the keys. As Krishnamurti himself once wrote:

Truth lies in observation of the content of the mind. Individuals build fences of security consisting of symbols, images, and beliefs. These images burden life and relationships. Our individuality is the name given to the form and superficial culture acquired from tradition and the environment. Freedom lies in freedom from the content of our consciousness. It is pure observation without direction, the choiceless awareness of our daily existence and activity.

After his stunning renunciation in the Netherlands, Krishnamurti returned to his beloved cottage in Ojai, California. In 1930 Krishnamurti finalized his break with Mrs. Besant by formally resigning from the Theosophical Society, although he continued to be supported by Mrs. Besant until her death in 1933. From then on Krishnamurti was, for the first time, on his own, and in the late thirties he began to earn a living by making lecture tours across the United States. Some of his followers had remained with him and organized his affairs, arranging speaking tours and publishing his talks. With the outbreak of the war in Europe, however, the American government sought to first draft Krishnamurti and then deport him, but due to a lack of available transport he was allowed to stay in California. Now forbidden by the authorities to speak in public and thereby deprived of his livelihood, Krishnamurti entered into a period of obscurity which lasted for almost a decade. During this time, Krishnamurti lived spartanly and alone, dividing his time between Ojai and a small cabin among the sequoias, supported only by occasional gifts from such famous friends as Aldous Huxley, Gerald Heard, and Christopher Isherwood (all followers of Vedanta, discussed below).

After the war, Krishnamurti slowly emerged as a low-key but immensely influential philosopher, popular with audiences in both the United States and his native India. In 1947 he finally returned to India, arriving two months after the independence of this country from Britain was declared. From then on, Krishnamurti divided his time between India, Europe, and the United States. Deeply interested in the problems and politics of India, he became a close friend to Indira Gandhi and her family in the 1970s. Krishnamurti also became highly interested in science and technology and was fascinated by the possibilities of artificial intelligence then being pioneered in the United States. At his death in 1986 at the age of ninety-one, Krishnamurti left behind a thriving foundation in Ojai to carry on his work. The Krishnamurti Foundation of America continues to function to this day, supporting such institutions as the Krishnamurti library and archives, and the Oak Grove elementary school.

Throughout its now almost century-long existence, Theosophy has continued to spawn new leaders, new organizations, and myriad splinter groups. In this chapter we have touched on only two Theosophical organizations which had an impact on California, but these were only two of many. Another famous Theosophical community, the Temple Home Association, functioned for a time during the first decade of this century on the outskirts of Pismo Beach; and yet another, the United Lodge of Theosophists, which began in 1909 in Monterey and San Francisco, continues to operate with twenty-two lodges today. Many groups based in California, such as Alice Bailey's Arcane School and the so-called I AM movement, while calling themselves Theosophist, became even more eclectic than perhaps Blavatsky intended and moved farther and farther away from the traditional South Asian religious thought that Blavatsky championed in the last decades of her life. Nevertheless, like Transcendentalists before them, these smaller Theosophical groups had their impact, serving as they did to expose more Californians—if indirectly—to the presuppositions of South Asian thought.

The World's Parliament of Religions and the Origins of American Vedanta

Theosophy was not the only South Asian-oriented religious movement which emerged in America during the vibrant last decades of the nineteenth century. Vedanta, as it was embodied in the Vedanta Societies and the Ramakrishna Mission, also became a popular religious alternative for Americans, especially in California. Unlike Theosophy, however, it is doubtful whether Vedanta would have been as successful if it had not been for that remarkable international gathering held in 1893 in Chicago called the World's Parliament of Religions.

Planned in conjunction with the Colombian Exposition, the World's Parliament of Religions was the brainchild of a Chicago Presbyterian minister, the Rev. John Henry Barrows. Barrows conceived the parliament as an opportunity to achieve world peace through greater cultural understanding. Delegations representing dozens of faiths (including Theosophy) were invited from around the world to come to present their beliefs to the world. In the month-long proceedings of the parliament, dozens of papers and addresses were delivered to enthusiastic overflow crowds, which included academics, divines, and the general public. At the conclusion of the parliament, the texts of all the papers presented were gathered together and published, along with photographs of the event, in two widely disseminated volumes.

Although the parliament was organized mainly by American Christians and had as one of the planks in its published platform that of defending "the impregnable foundation of Theism," the parliament also sought to take other religions seriously. Other planks in the platform stated that a goal of the parliament was to "show how many important truths [each religion] held in common," and to "inquire into what religions have contributed to each other." Thus, the parliament was held in a spirit of cooperation and comparison which, while it did not vouchsafe equality for every religion represented, at least gave it a voice. Debates over issues such as theism and immortality, while restrained and polite, were nevertheless serious and sustained, and had a lasting impact on many minds.

Indeed, some modern scholars of religion have argued, as has Robert S. Ellwood, that "the parliament did . . . much to encourage the development of comparative religion as an academic subject in American colleges and universities."

Of the many delegations to attend the parliament, the second largest (after the American) hailed from India. For the first time, Americans could hear about Indian religions from articulate, English-speaking practitioners of Hinduism, Jainism, Theravada Buddhism, and Zoroastrianism (Parsis). In papers such as "The Philosophy and Ethics of Jains" delivered by V.A. Gandhi and "Points of Resemblance and Differences Between Buddhism and Christianity" by the Theravada Buddhist, Anagarika Dharmapala, the American public was, perhaps for the first time, exposed to the broad spectrum of Indian religious belief. And many Americans responded with enthusiasm. As one scholar of American religion wrote: "To hear or to read firsthand the words of one immersed from birth in one of those fabled, primordial traditions to which Transcendentalism and Theosophy had, as it were, only pointed with awe from afar, was a momentous experience."

One of the superstars of the World's Parliament of Religions was a charismatic young Indian swami named Vivekananda (1863–1902). Dressed in a flamboyant turban and wearing a bright orange robe and red habit, Vivekananda's defense of Vedantic philosophy created quite an impression on his audience at the parliament. So too did Vivekananda's attitude toward things Western: university educated and an eloquent speaker of English, Vivekananda knew well how to appeal to American audiences. The goal of his coming, he boldly announced, was to cure the West of its spiritual poverty in exchange for the West's aid in curing the physical poverty of India. So powerful was his impact that well-wishers supplied him with enough funding to spend the next two years traveling throughout the United States, lecturing on Vedanta. During this time, Vivekananda founded Vedanta Societies in New York, San Francisco, Los Angeles, and Boston.

Vivekananda was the disciple of a famous rural Hindu saint, Ramakrishna (1836-86). Ramakrishna was a simple man whose Vedantic beliefs were straight out of medieval India. While remaining faithful to traditional Hinduism with its *bhakti* and *yoga*, Ramakrishna also advocated the use of devotional practices from other religions, such as Christianity and Islam. Indeed, Vivekananda used Ramakrishna's theme of tolerance as an opening to his Western audiences, and once the dialog had been opened, he would then straightforwardly present Ramakrishna's simple message. It contains three fundamental truths: first, men and women are naturally divine; second, the aim of life on earth is to discover the hidden God-head within; and third, that religious truths are universal. From this was derived a very simple ethic: that which is good in word and deed is that which aids in this divine discovery. Moreover, people must honor one another, for all are divine, and indeed, everyone's religious expression, no matter how unfamiliar or foreign, must be seen as an expression of this divinity.

After his success at the World's Parliament of Religions, Vivekananda decided to found an international fraternity based on Ramakrishna's message and devoted to missionary outreach. When he returned to India in 1897, Vivekananda founded the Ramakrishna Mission, an organization designed to supply the informal Vedanta centers which had sprung up in the United States since his visit with swamis and monks directly from India. The relationship between individual Vedanta centers and the Ramakrishna Mission centered in India remained informal, but it provided a highly workable framework for maintaining ties between the Mission and the American devotees of Ramakrishna, even after the early death of Vivekananda in 1902.

The format for teaching in each Vedanta center is a blend between East and West. Much time is spent in reading and in the classroom listening to lectures. Typically, Vedanta centers offer night-school courses during the week, most often focusing on the study of the Upanishads and the *Bhagavadgita*. Swamis also spend much of their time personally instructing students and charting their spiritual progress. No special spiritual techniques are advocated, nor is deep personal attachment to a *guru*. In contrast to Krishnamurti's teachings, however, devotion to a *guru* is deemed licit, but remains an individual choice. Too much dependence on the teacher is nevertheless seen as dangerous.

While the Vedanta of Vivekananda is a highly westernized and intellectualized approach to Hinduism, the cultural context of Hinduism is not entirely forgotten. In this, Vedanta differs from most Theosophical organizations, which tended to downplay or dispense altogether with the ritual aspect of South Asian religions. From the beginning, many Vedanta centers offered in their temples a regular schedule of ritual practices. *Arati* (the offering of fire), for example, is today performed daily in most Vedanta temples, and on special days of the Hindu lunar calendar, *puja* and *bhajan*s (devotional hymns) are conducted.

Throughout the decades and up to the present, the Vedanta Society in the United States has evidenced a slow but steady growth. Since the beginning of the movement, the Ramakrishna Mission has had a strong presence in Southern California, and many of the earliest Vedanta centers are found there. During the twenties and thirties, Vedanta was especially popular among the movie and literary circles, and such well-known California residents as Gerald Heard, Aldous Huxley, and Christopher Isherwood were deeply involved. In addition, the main organizational center for the Ramakrishna Mission came to be located in Los Angeles, and the Vedanta Press in Hollywood was, until the 1960s, one of the major sources for Hindu texts and literature in the United States. The Mission also maintains convent/monasteries in Hollywood and Santa Barbara, as well as a monastery in Orange County.

Twentieth-Century Developments

In the first part of this chapter we have dealt with several Western religious movements which emerged in response to South Asian religious ideas. It must be pointed out, however, that the birth of these movements occurred in an environment which rejected the larger Indian culture from which these ideas came. In some cases, such as Transcendentalism and early Theosophy, it must also be admitted that the approach to South Asian ideas was heavily influenced by an unreflective racism. Emerson, for example, once described the scale of moral evolution as ascending from dog to "Hottentot" to, eventually, "a Massachusetts man." And indeed, even Blavatsky's original concept of human spiritual evolution was heavily tinged with racial overtones and cultural bias:

> Man's evolvement takes him through seven root races, each of which has seven subraces. The first three root races perfect the union of matter and spirit; the fourth expresses the union, the last three represent the struggle of the spirit to be free of matter. We now live in the Fifth Root Race. The third race was the Lemurian, so named for a mythical submerged continent in the Pacific Ocean, and the fourth was the Atlantean, so named for Atlantis, the paradisical origin of man. The Fifth Root Race, the Aryan, finds its culmination in the Anglo-Saxon subrace. From this point, mankind will evolve into spiritual adepts. [Melton (1978): 136]

It is interesting to note as well that when Besant and Leadbetter settled on a native Indian, Krishnamurti, as the World Teacher, the first order of business was to Westernize him as much as possible, or, in the words of one biographer, to see that he was "stripped of all Indianness." Krishnamurti was dressed in Western fashion, ate only Western food, and was forbidden to speak any language save English. Since the pinnacle of human development was the Western gentleman, it was felt that it would not do for the World Teacher to seem too Indian.

Even when racism was not such an issue, there still operated a not-so-subtle presumption that Europeans and Americans could somehow improve or perfect these South Asian religious systems by Westernizing them. The Ramakrishna Mission represented a more culturally contextualized presentation of Hinduism than Americans had previously responded to, but still its appeal was largely intellectual, with its lectures and classes and highly self-conscious emphasis on philosophy before practice and personality. As one historian of religion acutely observed:

The Theosophical and Vedanta preeminence meant the preponderance of a highly verbal and intellectual style, based, for most people, on reading books and hearing lectures. The idea content was Eastern in large part, though under heavy syncretistic or modernizing tendencies. But the practical or worship and sociological forms of expression of these groups were reassuringly familiar to Americans drawn eastward by books and thoughts of the Transcendentalist sort. One might have heard lectures in the Chautauqua style, or in the case of Vedanta witnessed a simple service with a rather cerebral sermon reminiscent of liberal Protestantism. In both cases, symbols of continuity with American culture and religiosity in the style of worship and institution shared center stage with ideas from far away.

It was not until the watershed decade of the sixties that large numbers of Americans felt comfortable with both the religious ideas *and* the religious culture of India.

Late Twentieth Century

Post World War II America presented an entirely different climate for Eastern religions. A new appreciation of cultural pluralism was emerging in intellectual circles. Changes in immigration quotas after 1965 greatly increased the number of people coming to the United States from Asia, thereby increasing intercultural interaction on a daily basis and diminishing the stereotype of the "exotic

Oriental." The war itself did much to shape a new openness to non-Western cultural traditions. The atrocities committed by Westerners against members of their own modern industrial culture had undermined people's belief in modern Western nations as the natural culmination of human social evolution. "Man's inhumanity to man" seemed to indicate a moral void in Western culture. These factors contributed to the exploration of Eastern traditions as an alternative source of spirituality in the 1960s. Nowhere was this new interest in alternative religions more prominent than in California.

Self-Realization Fellowship

One of the teachers who laid a foundation for the later popularization of Hindu practices was Paramahansa Yogananda (1893–1952). Yogananda arrived in the United States in 1920 to give lectures on Hinduism. In 1935, he founded the Self-Realization Fellowship as a vehicle for his teaching mission. Unlike the mostly philosophical emphasis of the Vedanta Society, he focused on the traditional practices of *yoga*. He taught that each person has an inner divine self and an inherent capacity for divine joy and love, but because of ignorance we misdirect our efforts toward outer things in the material world. He instructed his followers in a specific technique, called Kriya Yoga, to redirect their energy from outward things toward inner awareness of the true nature of the self. Yogananda adapted the vocabularies of Western psychology, science, and Christianity to explain his teachings. He used them to demonstrate that the ancient wisdom of *yoga* was in accord with the latest findings of Western science and had empirical and experiential validity. He also taught that *yoga* philosophy was the underlying essence of all religions. These ideas about the scientific nature and universality of *yoga* philosophy and his successful use of published works established a model that other teachers later emulated.

Today the Self-Realization Fellowship has branches all over the world, including India. The headquarters for the Fellowship in the United States is in Los Angeles, and there are nine centers in California. Swami Yogananda is recognized throughout the state of California, even by those who have no interest in Asian religions, because there are copies of his autobiography on the shelves of almost every bookstore, new or used, in the state. In west Los Angeles there is a beautifully landscaped park called the "Lake Shrine" that has lotus towers, a windmill, and some of the ashes of Mahatma Gandhi, whom Yogananda had initiated into Kriya Yoga. The Fellowship consists of laity and renunciates. The latter have gone through an introductory series of more than fifty lessons and practice Kriya Yoga. They meditate at least two hours every day and live a monastic life. The present head of the Fellowship is a nun named Daya Mata, who presides over a governing board of eight long-time members. The Fellowship continues to gain new followers even though Yogananda died in 1952.

Self-Realization Fellowship services, which are held in small chapels, draw people from all age groups. The use of a combined cross and lotus symbol and the pictures of saints from non-Hindu traditions that accompany the image of Yogananda give evidence of the belief that these teachings are the underlying reality of all faiths. The meetings begin with chanting and include talks that may draw on scriptures from both East and West. This syncretism is deliberate and wholly in accord with Yogananda's teachings. Yogananda established an image of the *yogi* as a teacher of an ancient wisdom directly applicable to life in a modern scientific world. This image of the *yogi* has affected other Indian religious movements in the West.

Transcendental Meditation

In the 1960s, an Indian teacher named Maharishi Mahesh Yogi popularized a simplified meditation technique called Transcendental Meditation. The Maharishi came to the United States in 1959 and used modern media to gain the publicity necessary to spread his teachings. He appeared on talk shows, hired PR men and courted famous personalities. TM became part of the hippie culture, and even the Beatles were meditators for a while. The basic teaching of TM states that it is possible to enjoy life to the fullest by getting to the ground of joy through meditation. Transcendental Meditation is supposed to be a natural process. It does not involve practices of asceticism or *yoga* postures that work against the normal functioning of the body. It is a process of following the thoughts that arise in the mind back to their ultimate source, or exploring beneath phenomenal reality to make contact with the underlying, changeless Consciousness. This is achieved by meditating with the aid of a *mantra*, a scared utterance, given to the practitioner at the time of his initiation.

The popularity of the movement with the counter-culture in the 1960s provoked a somewhat negative reaction to meditation in the mainstream. Other image problems arose when the Beatles became disenchanted after visiting the Maharishi's training center at Rishikesh in India, when the master was seen riding in chauffered limosines, and a speaking-concert tour with a rock group went awry. Then, in the 1970s, TM gained new popularity, but this time among urban business and professional people. It was now presented as a scientific means to reduce stress and enhance creativity and peace of mind. The Maharishi also teaches that large numbers of meditators can affect the state of the world, claiming that if just ten percent of the people in the world would meditate, there would be no war.

This shift from counter-culture to stress-aid marks a change in the status of Indian religious practices in the United States. Where once Vedantic philosophy had a small following among an intellectual elite, practices of *yoga* and meditation have become part of the mainstream. These practices entered the country under the tutelage of the religious seekers of the 1960s, accompanied by claims about the miraculous powers of wonder-working holy men. Such claims inspired scientific testing of brain waves and heart rates in meditators. These studies resulted in acceptance of meditation as a legitimate means of affecting one's physiological and mental state, but, in the process, the practices were divorced from their original religious context. They could now be incorporated into non-Indian traditions, or practiced as part of a stress reduction program without any religious implications at all. Most of the people who practice TM do so as part of their spiritual life, but the transition in the emphasis used to popularize the tradition demonstrates a changed attitude toward *yoga* and meditation in America.

Saiva Siddhanta Church

The shape of Hinduism in California during the next decades will be affected by some remarkable changes in the attitudes of non-Indians. In the nineteenth and early twentieth centuries, when Americans first took an interest in Eastern philosophy, they ignored the culture and popular religious practices of the traditions from which these philosophies were drawn. That changed dramatically in the 1960s. During that decade, Americans began to travel to India and learn about the daily practices of Hinduism as well as the ancient philosophies. At first, they brought home mystical practices of yogic postures and meditation techniques to facilitate a quest for spiritual knowledge. Gradually, a few Americans developed an appreciation of full-scale Hindu *dharma*.

One such group of American Hindus can be found in the Saiva Siddhanta Church. The organization was founded by Subramaniya, a native Californian, who traveled to Sri Lanka, where he was initiated by Siva Yogaswami in 1949. He returned to the United States and spent many years continuing his spiritual discipline before founding the Subramaniya Yoga Order in 1957. Eventually the headquarters was moved to Hawaii, and in the 1970s the order was renamed the Saiva Siddhanta Church. The teachings of the organization are based on the South Indian Shaivite traditions. In their temples, the devotees honor Shiva *lingams* as embodiments of the Lord, and most families have household shrines where the deity may be invoked in daily *pujas*. The church has a strong following in the San Francisco Bay area, which includes both South Asian and Anglo Americans.

The Saiva Siddhanta Church in Concord is organized like an American church. It is situated in a complex of four Spanish-style buildings and includes a temple, a cultural hall, a kitchen, children's school, and monastery. The church has a resident priest for the temple and also has seven associate pastors, called Adiyars. The Adiyars, who give lectures every night and sermons on Sundays, are family men who have been formally trained to serve as clergy. The Saiva community is particularly pleased with the inclusion of classroom space where their children can receive a Hindu education. For their part, the children say they are happy to be part of a circle of young folks who share the same culture and religion, since they found it difficult to explain Hindu traditions to their peers in public schools. The church even sponsors its own Hindu Boy Scout troop, so that their children may combine their religion with mainstream American activities.

This American-Hindu tradition has formulated some other interesting ways to fit its religion into its cultural setting. For example, some of the families in the San Francisco Bay area were concerned that their children were feeling left out of the holiday celebrations during the Christmas season, for in spite of the American ideal of separation of church and state, many of the public school holidays are oriented around the Christian calendar. These families therefore drew on existing Hindu traditions to find an alternative celebration for their children. In parts of India, the winter solstice is associated with Ganesha, the elephant-headed god who helps people overcome obstacles. The Bay Area Saivas established a five-day celebration of the five-headed Ganesha, which culminates on December 25. The families set up temporary shrines to Ganesha in their living rooms, decorated with pine bows and ornaments, and use this as a means to contemplate the love and compassion of the deity. On December 25 they have a large gathering at which all the children receive presents.

Although the need to find a substitute for Christmas indicates the continuing influence of the American Christian mainstream, the presence of American converts who embrace traditional Hinduism, complete with reverence for temple images as physical embodiments of the presence of God, suggests that a greater appreciation of non-Christian religions is emerging in California. While in the first half of the century Americans were intrigued by Eastern philosophy, now they are gaining a greater understanding of the religious contexts of those philosophies. This greater respect for the religious milieu of ideas about *karma*, rebirth, and the underlying unity of existence may in turn make it easier for Asian-Indian Americans to adapt their ancestral traditions to life in the Golden State.

Sikh Dharma Brotherhood

Americans have also become followers of the Sikh tradition. Harbhajan Singh Puri, a Punjabi Sikh, came to Los Angeles in the late 1960s and began to teach *yoga*. He attracted a group of young followers out of the counterculture and soon set up his own center. In 1969, the teacher, now known as Yogi Bhajan, established the Healthy, Happy, Holy Organization. In the early 1970s, Yogi Bhajan led his followers to become linked with the Sikh religion. He took a group of eighty-four disciples on a visit to the Golden Temple in Amritsar, where he was honored for his "missionary work" by the Punjabi Sikhs. In 1973, he founded the Sikh Dharma Brotherhood, and his followers were initiated into Sikhism.

Yogi Bhajan's teachings are a combination of yogic and Sikh doctrine and practices. Followers practice yogic chanting, meditation, and breathing exercises, as well as reverence for their spiritual teacher. These individualistic meditation practices are balanced by Sikh ideas about community and living religiously in worldly life. The American converts adopted the outward symbols of Sikh identity; both men and women wear white Punjabi clothing and turbans. Many of the American converts live in communal *ashram*s, the largest of which is the international headquarters for the organization in Los Angeles. The organization is quite small outside of California.

Although the American converts were greeted enthusiastically at first by the Punjabi Sikhs, relations between the two groups have grown strained because of the fundamental difference in their sense of Sikh identity. For the American converts, Sikhism is a religion. They criticized the Punjabi immigrants for becoming "Westernized" and leaving behind the symbols of the Khalsa, like the beard and turban, in their efforts to adapt to their American environment. The converts also tended to make distinctions between Punjabi practices they considered cultural, such as ideas about the role of women, and "true Sikhism." Thus, they seemed to be claiming that they were the true Sikhs. But for the Indian immigrants, Sikhism is very much a part of their cultural identity and deeply bound to preservation of heritage. The American converts accepted the religion and followed many of the practices, but they could not speak Punjabi or read the Punjabi script (*gurmukhi*, the language of the *Adi Granth*). They also had practices that were not in accord with Punjabi customs. The women wore turbans just like the men, and young married women wore white, which in the Punjab is reserved for widows and religious leaders. The converts may have been Sikhs, but they were not Punjabis.

These tensions were aggravated by the conflict in the Punjab. American converts have not taken part in the protests of the government attack on the Golden Temple. The converts have preferred to emphasize the religious aspects of Sikhism and avoid involvement in the political affairs of the Punjab, but this has led Punjabi Sikhs to see them as outsiders rather than members of the Sikh brotherhood. The conflicts that have strengthened the cohesion of the Punjabi immigrant community have also worked to create barriers between the Sikhs and their American brethren.

There are attempts to maintain contacts between the two factions, and in regions where the Punjabi immigrant community is small, cooperative activities are common. It is where larger numbers of both groups reside that the cultural differences emerge. In Los Angeles, members of the Sikh Dharma Brotherhood who once took part in services at the regular Sikh *gurdwara* have ceased to interact with the Punjabis and have set up their own religious center. This pattern has been repeated throughout the state. The Sikh Dharma Brotherhood is now a movement in decline, and there is little chance that the membership will grow as long as Sikh identity means being Punjabi. Perhaps only after the political conflict in the Punjab is resolved will there be an opportunity for Sikhs to decide if they are going to once again embrace converts from other cultures.

Buddhism

Openness to converts is a hallmark of Buddhism, dating back to the era of the Buddha himself, who sent teachers out to preach in vernacular languages so all might have access to his Dhamma. The early American interest in Buddhism naturally focused on the Mahayana traditions of East Asia, carried to the United States by Chinese and Japanese immigrants. Study of Buddhism began as a field for intellectuals who focused on philosophy, with little concern for popular daily practices, but gradually Buddhist meditation practices have become part of American culture. Buddhism has had a particularly strong presence in California throughout the twentieth century. This began with the influence of Chinese and Japanese immigrants, but in the last three decades Theravada Buddhists from Sri Lanka and Southeast Asia have begun to make an impact on American Buddhism. Tibetan Buddhist teachers have also come to California. Today, Americans are taking up the practices of Theravada and Tibetan Buddhism, just as they previously adopted ideas from the East Asian Buddhist traditions.

Perhaps the first Americans to take up the path of Theravada Buddhism were Jack Kornfield and Joseph Goldstein. Both went to Asia as Peace Corps volunteers and studied intensively with Theravadin teachers. Goldstein studied at Bodhgaya, in India, with Anagarika Munindra, who was himself a disciple of Mahasi Sayadaw in Burma. Kornfield took the vows of a monk and spent years at the forest hermitage of the Thai teacher Achaan Chaa. There he was required to follow the full regimen of the traditional Buddhist renunciate, just as the Thai monks did.

When Kornfield came back to the United States, he decided to return to lay life because it was impossible to keep the vows of a forest monk while living in America. Goldstein also returned to the United States, and the two Westerners, with their traditional training, met while teaching Theravada meditation classes at the Tibetan Buddhist Naropa Institute in Colorado. Joseph and Jack, as they are called by their students, teamed up to continue teaching and founded the Insight Meditation Center in Massachusetts in 1976. The center was run by the members of the community who lived there, rather than being built around the charisma of its founders, like most other American meditation centers. Within a few years, Theravada elders such as Angarika Munindra and Mahasi Sayadaw were coming from Asia to visit the American center.

Insight Meditation West in Woodacre is the California branch of the Insight Meditation Center. It began as an informal organization and has since grown considerably. Jack Kornfield also established the Dharma Foundation in Oakland in 1982. Both centers offer people on the West Coast a chance to study Theravada Buddhist teachings and to work with meditation instructors. They also provide a setting for one-day or weekend meditation sittings, as well as retreats, which can last from one to three weeks. The people taking part in these practices are mostly middle-class Americans of all ages. Some are interested in Buddhism for religious reasons, while others believe meditation can improve health and mental function. The teachings and practices at the centers have been adapted to American life. The Western teachers are layfolk, not monks, and the students who come to study are taking temporary breaks from their householder lives rather than embarking on a traditional monastic life. Goldstein once stated that he thought they might be starting a lineage that would be preserved outside the monastic continuum, and would thus become a new experience of the unfolding of the Dhamma, the Buddha's teachings. This modified Theravada practice has been approved by the traditional teachers, who acknowledge that some rules are not appropriate in some settings. It is this flexibility in the Buddhist tradition, a flexibility seen in the willingness to translate texts into any language and adapt teachings to cultural settings, that allows Buddhism to spread so easily.

The same adaptation has been evident in the Tibetan Buddhist traditions that are now part of California culture. The Tibetan teachers have insisted on preserving the traditional form of the teachings and meditation practices, but have adapted their teaching formats to meet the needs of a lay audience drawn from American society. Classes are offered on weekends, and Buddhist practices are adapted to householder lifestyles. Extended study may be done in retreats and intensive summer courses, but students are not required to become monks or move into monasteries. The Tibetan teachers have incorporated Western theories of psychology and science into their explanations of Buddhist practice to make their instructions more comprehensible to their Western students. In the process, they are creating an American sect of Vajrayana Buddhism that can be preserved and passed on by their Western students.

Conclusion

The American approach to South Asian religions has gone through a process of evolution. The early interest in Hindu and Buddhist philosophy that contributed to the formation of Western traditions like Theosophy has gradually been transformed into a real appreciation for the richness of the Asian religions. The first Western intellectuals who traveled in India and Sri Lanka appropriated Asian spirituality and used it to answer Western questions about human potential and life. They took up ideas of the perfectability of the individual self through knowledge of the Supreme Truth, but disregarded all the native traditions of worship and devotion. Then the spiritual quest of the counterculture brought a greater awareness of

South Asian religious practices of *yoga*, meditation, and devotion to personal gods. Claims about the benefits of *yoga* and meditation were verified by laboratory studies, and these practices became part of American culture. In the process, however, they were often divorced from their religious meanings. Although the religious centers that teach South Asian traditions in the United States include instruction in *yoga* and meditation, most Americans do not think of these practices as part of Asian religion. Today they are regarded as secular physical and mental systems to be used for exercise and stress reduction.

The appropriation of Eastern spirituality did not stop with practices such as *yoga* and meditation. It also brought different ideas about the nature of God and the meaning of human life to a generation that was no longer satisfied with modern urban life. People were rejecting the modern theory that described the universe as a machine, separate from the human observer, and embracing the idea of an integrated, holistic universe. South Asian religions offered ideas compatible with this new emphasis, ideas like reincarnation, *karma*, and the pervasive presence of the Brahman, which is both the material and causal source of creation, and also the inner nature of the individual. The idea of a perfect inner self that could be realized through self-effort and yogic discipline was adopted by the human potential movement. On a purely spiritual level, people took up Eastern practices seeking mystical religious experiences that were no longer emphasized in Western religions. Fostered by these two groups, the spiritual seekers and the psychologists interested in human potential, South Asian religious ideas became part of mainstream American awareness.

The large college populations of the San Francisco Bay area and Los Angeles area brought a wide range of Asian religious teachers and practitioners to the West Coast. Young people went to Asia looking for enlightenment in the 1960s and 1970s and brought back teachings and teachers. Hindu swamis and Buddhist monks made tours of the United States and set up centers where students could meet to study and practice their instructions. During the first decade, their following was mostly limited to the counterculture, but by the late 1970s and the 1980s, the appeal of Asian religions had spread beyond the college crowd, and today people from every age group and social class may be found taking part in Hindu, Sikh, and Buddhist traditions.

In California, Eastern terms and ideas have become part of everyday language. Everyone knows words like *karma, mantra, yoga,* reincarnation, *nirvana,* and Buddha. Most of these words have become so common that they are no longer italicized by American publishers. South Asian religions have also provided one of the primary sources for ideas used by the "New Age" movements that are so prevalent in California. New Age groups draw on a wide variety of sources, including Native American traditions, but many of the foundational emphases, such as past-life research, vegetarianism, meditation practices, and healing techniques, derive from South Asia. Most New Age groups are spiritual, but in a way they are practicing a cultural imperialism similar to that of the early twentieth century because they appropriate ideas from other religions and lift them from their traditional contexts.

Despite this continued tendency to borrow only bits and pieces, there has been a change in the way many Westerners approach South Asian religions. The years have brought greater understanding of and respect for South Asian cultures to enrich knowledge of the religious traditions among Western practitioners. Furthermore, the South Asian teachers coming west have learned to adapt their instructions to their international audiences. As this process unfolds American adherents are gaining an appreciation of the richness of the traditional practices, including a greater understanding of temple worship and the importance of the temple image for devotional sects, a practice which once was automatically dismissed as idolatry. At the same time as the Americans are learning to understand the daily practices of South Asian religions, the South Asian religious leaders are modifying their traditions to meet the needs of urbanizing cultures in Asia and among the Asian American community. The new teachings they are bringing to their transplanted communities are accessible to both Asian Americans and Euro-Americans. So, in the late twentieth century, the South Asian religious traditions that came to California by way of Western intellectuals borrowing from Asian wisdom and were later augmented by counterculture interest in *yoga* and meditation have now laid the foundation for better Western understanding of the traditions being practiced by the South Asian immigrant community. In California, East and West have indeed met.

Bibliography

Albanese, Catherine L. *America: Religions and Religion*, 2nd Edition. Belmont, CA: Wadsworth Publishing Co., 1992.

Christy, Arthur. *The Orient in American Transcendentalism: A Study of Emerson, Thoreau, and Alcott*. New York: Octagon Books, 1963.

Ellwood, Robert S. (editor). *Eastern Spirituality in America: Selected Writings*. New York: Paulist Press, 1987.

Ellwood, Robert S. and Partin, Harry B. *Religious and Spiritual Groups in Modern America*. New Jersey: Prentice Hall, Englewood Cliffs, 1988.

Francis, E. V. *Emerson and Hindu Scriptures*. Cochin: Academic Publications, 1972.

Gomes, Michael. *The Dawning of the Theosophical Movement*. Wheaton, Ill: Theosophical Publishing House, 1987.

Greenwalt, Emmett A. *The Point Loma Community, 1897–1942: A Theosophical Experiment*. Berkeley: University of California Press, 1955.

Hine, Robert V. *California's Utopian Colonies*. San Marino, CA: The Huntington Library, 1953.

Jayakar, Pupul. *Krishnamurti, A Biography*. San Francisco, CA: Harper & Row, Publishers, 1988.

Lancaster, Clay. *The Incredible World's Parliament of Religions at the Chicago Columbian Exposition of 1893: A Comparative and Critical Study*. Fonwell, England: Centaur Press, 1987.

Melton, J. Gordon. *The Encyclopedia of American Religions*, 3rd Edition. Detroit, MI: Gale Research Inc., 1989.

Stein, William Bysshe. *Two Brahman Sources of Emerson and Thoreau*. Gainesville, FL: Scholar's Facsimilies & Reprints, 1967.

6 Conclusion

This book is by no means a complete record of the South Asian religious traditions in California. It has focused on the three largest traditions indigenous to South Asia—Sikhism, Hinduism, and Buddhism—and only mentioned Jains, Muslims, Zoroastrians, Christians, and Jews in passing, even though all these traditions are practiced by immigrants from this region. Islam, Christianity, and Judaism are not specifically South Asian religions, and, consequently, members of these faiths have had quite different experiences in California. They have been able to join congregations where they are part of a larger international community of the faithful, and have not had the same struggle to transplant an entirely new religion onto foreign soil. The Indian Zoroastrians (Parsis), who also form part of an international community with their Iranian brethren, have a temple in the eastern United States but have had very little impact on California. Jainism is, of course, a purely Indian religion, but it too has left little impression on the California religious landscape. Most Jains worship in small groups, which gather in private homes, or go to Hindu temples. Hopefully it will be possible to add information on the California Jains to a later edition of this book.

The religious traditions which have been described in this book demonstrate a wide diversity in the ways different religions are transplanted by different types of communities. The Sikhs, who were the first to arrive in California in significant numbers, came from a close-knit agricultural community, which they were able to recreate in the central valleys of the Golden State. The Sikh *gurus*, especially Guru Gobind Singh, organized their religion in such a way as to affirm group identity during years of armed conflict with oppressive rulers. This established a clear identity between religion and the community. The immigrants were able to draw on their religious faith as a way to meet their need to establish cultural identity in a strange land.

Furthermore, the format of the Sikh tradition makes it portable. A Sikh *gurdwara* may be set up anyplace a copy of the *Guru Granth Sahib* is kept with proper honor, and any Sikh who has the ability to read the *gurmukhi* script is qualified to lead services. The early Sikh immigrants brought a copy of the *Guru Granth Sahib* to California and set up the first American *gurdwara* in Stockton in 1912. The tradition almost died out because there weren't enough Sikh women to preserve the family practices and language, but revised immigration laws after 1948 allowed the Punjabis to send for wives and families and fully recreate their traditional kinship networks in California. Sikhs continue to maintain their own separate communities in the agricultural regions of Central California even as new immigrants and second-generation Sikhs spread to urban areas. But whether they remain in their traditional farming occupations or join the rush of the city, the Sikhs always retain their sense of belonging to a religious and cultural community.

The Hindus, on the other hand, have come from diverse regional cultures with myriad religious sects and, despite early efforts to form ecumenical Hindu organizations, the greater the number of Hindus, the greater the tendency to divide up along regional lines. Most of the Hindu immigrants came to California after 1965, when changes in immigration policy gave preference to educated professionals and people with technical skills. These immigrants, coming from urban areas of India and countries in Africa and the Caribbean, were no longer part of a village-kinship structure like that of the Punjabis. They did not have the same life-long connections with their neighbors in India and did not come to the United States in groups based on old relationships. Hence, they had to form new connections in their new land. In America, they settled in areas that offered economic and educational opportunities, usually in the suburbs, where they had few connections to other South Asians. Despite the scattered settlement pattern, these Hindus joined together to form cultural societies. Their success in achieving middle-class status through their English fluency and high educations, without going through a process of assimilation to American culture, helped bolster their appreciation of their own traditions. The desire to preserve their cultural heritage was strengthened when they began to start families and wanted to raise their children with good, traditional values.

Religious centers and temples were built largely to help preserve the Hindu tradition for the second generation. But Hinduism proved difficult to transplant to a new land since it is intimately connected with the land of India. Indian temples are tied to a rich mythology, which describes how the gods enter the world to interact with their devotees. These gods had not previously visited the shores of the United States, but now there are consecrated images in the California Hindu temples, clay images of Ganesha have been submerged in San Francisco Bay, and a Shiva *lingam* has manifested itself in Golden Gate Park. California still lacks wandering renunciates and holy men, but there are priests performing traditional rituals at the temples and children are studying language, dance, and religion at cultural camps. This second generation has far less attachment to regional-linguistic identities and prefers to think of itself as "Indian," so the tendency for the community to divide along regional lines may be reversed when the Americanized Indians gain dominance.

There have been some major changes in the structure of communal religious life in the United States. At an institutional level, there are changes in scheduling and temple governance. In India, ceremonies are held according to a lunar calendar, but here services are shifted to weekends to accommodate work schedules. American temples do not have landholdings to provide their maintenance incomes, so the South Asians are adapting to the need to arrange sponsorship to support their temples. It is easier to convince people to donate to construction projects than to arrange regular tithes for yearly upkeep, and some Hindus fear that there are now more temples than the communities can sustain. In California, donations to religious centers have become a status symbol for many wealthy Hindus, but the second generation may be less inclined to compete for status in this way because they give less importance to the traditional externals of Hinduism. The financial stability of the temples is, therefore, an ongoing concern.

There have also been changes in personal religion. Practices that seem incomprehensible or outdated, such as the long Vedic ceremonies, are being dropped, especially by the second generation. The young folks prefer intellectual ideas of a formless deity over reverence for temple images and have little use for rituals that are not clearly applicable to modern life. Perhaps the greatest change of all is the disappearance of folk practices. To some extent this shift simply reflects the social class of the immigrants. They are educated urbanites, not traditional villagers, and have little need to offer prayers in appeasement of the goddess of smallpox when they can immunize their children and go to hospitals. Their prayers are directed to the great deities, not the folk divinities. The temples of California have images of Vishnu, Shiva, and Devi, but there are no village boundary shrines dedicated to a community's protective goddess, no tombs where people may pray to deified heroes and sainted wives. The Hindus of California are emphasizing the aspects of their traditions that are appropriate for the modern lifestyle of educated, middle-class Americans, and leaving behind practices that no longer fit their lives.

A similar process is evident among South Asian Buddhists in California. Many of the localized folk traditions are disappearing, especially among the American-educated second generation, who learn their Buddhism in Sunday school classes rather than through daily village life. Religious education is in the hands of trained monks, who have preserved the texts and commentaries that describe Lord Buddha's philosophy and practices for more than two thousand years. They teach a more philosophical Buddhism, with less emphasis on devotion to Buddha, than the faith of the old village culture.

Despite the antiquity of its teachings, Buddhism is an adaptable tradition because it is a missionary religion and its educated monks are willing to translate their teachings into new languages in order to spread the Dhamma and the Buddhist practices. Yet because the Buddhists in California are from different countries with their own popular traditions and cultural practices, they generally prefer to establish separate temples and keep monks from their own traditions to serve the immigrant communities. The Buddhists are also divided by social class differences. Those who came from Sri Lanka are mostly educated, English speakers who have been able to move into the American middle class. The refugees from Southeast Asia have had a harder time. A few are educated elites, but the majority are poor farmers who could not read their own languages, let alone English. Some of these refugees are now stuck in ethnic ghettos, but even when they live in poverty, the community pools its resources to support a few monks.

The Buddhist centers offer classes on Buddhist texts and individualized meditation instruction for those who wish to spend some time following the practices traditionally reserved for monks. Many of these classes are now offered in English, in an effort to reach out to the larger American public. This adoption of English will undoubtedly help make Buddhism accessible to the Americanized children of these immigrants. The effort to spread the Buddhist Dhamma to Americans is even more evident among the Tibetan teachers who are traveling to the United States especially to teach Westerners.

The American interest in Buddhism and other Asian religions reflects the changing climate for immigrant traditions in California. The different experiences of the Sikhs, Hindus, and Buddhists in California are the result of local cultural changes as well as the backgrounds of the immigrants and the institutional forms of their religions. When the Sikhs first arrived at the beginning of the twentieth century, they were part of a frontier labor force in competition with other workers. At that time, American interest in Asian religion was limited to a few intellectuals who focused on philosophy and ignored popular religious practices. Naturally, there was no interaction between these intellectuals and the Sikh laborers.

By the time the Hindus and Buddhists who arrived after 1965 began to establish religious centers in California, the cultural climate had changed. Theosophy, the Vedanta Society, and Yogananda's Self Realization Fellowship had made South Asian ideas part of middle-class conversation. The 1960s youth movement had brought Asian religious practices to middle-class America, and words like *yoga*, *karma*, and *nirvana* had become part of the California vocabulary. This was also the era of a rising appreciation for cultural pluralism that nicely complimented a slowly improving knowledge of the cultural contexts that went with each tradition. Simultaneously, this emphasis on pluralism helped legitimize Sikh, Hindu, and Buddhist efforts to preserve their cultural identities in their new land.

Yet acceptance of cultural pluralism does not guarantee understanding of multiple cultures. Most Californians know very little about the lifestyles and beliefs of their neighbors. Few non-Asians know why the orange-clad monks walk through their neighborhood in Hollywood or why Sikh men wear turbans, even though robed monks and turbaned men are now common sights throughout the state. Often ignorance of each other's cultures from both sides creates problems. There have been protests against proposed Hindu temples in residential neighborhoods because of fears of noise and traffic. These are usually resolved through simple communication when the Hindus learn what the concerns are and make plans to address them in revised plans. Religious symbols have also caused problems. There was an uproar when a Buddhist center placed swastikas on its fences, apparently without realizing what the reaction to this emblem might be. The word *swastika* means "good for-tune, auspiciousness" in Sanskrit, and the symbol was in use in South Asia for thousands of years before the Nazis borrowed it. Community outrage over the fences surprised the monks, but the conflict led to some educational dialog that helped establish rela-tions between the larger population and the new religious center. Sikhs and South Asian Muslims have had problems because they are often associated with Middle Eastern terrorists due to the unfor-tunate tendency of the media to label such people as "Muslim" ter-rorists. When tensions are high, all American Muslims, regardless of ancestral ethnicity, brace themselves for trouble, and often the Sikhs are harassed by those who think they are Muslims. These con-flicts show how little knowledge Californians have of the diverse cultures that make up the population of the Golden State.

The process of improving knowledge on both sides is, however, progressing. Various organizations that provide services to commu-nities with large numbers of South Asians are asking for instruction in cultural traditions so they will better be able to meet the needs of the people. For example, medical workers in the central valleys of California are being trained to understand attitudes toward the body and health among Indians, especially women. Schools are often the places where the most intensive accommodation of plural-ism takes place as parents strive to find a balance between main-taining traditions for their children and having them learn all that they will need to succeed in life. Schools have amended rules pro-hibiting hats to make room for turbans and have changed physical education dress codes to allow more modest attire for girls, such as sweatpants instead of shorts.

The adaptations being made on both sides may be illustrated by a recent court ruling involving Sikh school children. Three Sikh boys had been banned from attending school because they wore *kir-pans*, the small daggers that have become the symbol of the sword Guru Gobind Singh instructed all members of the Khalsa to wear, and because they refused to stop wearing them when told to by school officials. The U.S. Court of Appeals for the Ninth Circuit in San Francisco ruled that they could return to classes and that the Livingston School District had to accommodate the Sikh religious beliefs. The court pointed out that the daggers were not weapons, and other districts in the state allow the daggers if their tips are blunted and they are bolted into their sheaths. Such a ruling would have been unlikely in the first part of the twentieth century. At that time, the Sikhs in California were willing to give up the external symbols of their faith in order to survive in an unfriendly state, and the Anglo-Californians had so little knowledge of South Asian religions that they dubbed all South Asians "Hindoos." Today, the Sikhs are middle-class Americans who proudly wear the symbols of their religion and pass on that religion to their children. In the same way, Hindus and Buddhists are carrying on their religious practices and educating their children in traditional values. And here at the end of the twentieth century, most Californians know that Sikhism, Hinduism, and Buddhism are three separate traditions, three of the myriad faiths that make up the religious contours of California.

Index

141